ANCIENT GREECE

Based on the travels of
Aristoboulos of Athens

Compiled by Lesley Sims and Conrad Mason

Illustrated by Ian Mcnee,
Ian Jackson & Inklink-Firenze

Designed by Marc Maynard

Dear reader,

This book is inspired by my first visit to Ancient Greece. It was a pretty scary experience, but since then, I've been back many times, and made pages and pages of notes on this fascinating civilization.

Some good friends of mine — Lesley Sims and Conrad Mason — have helped me turn my notes into the book you're holding now.

I hope it's useful...

Aristoboulos of Athens*

*This isn't my real name — it's the one I use when I'm in Ancient Greece. I have so many names these days, I've almost lost count. But they help me get by in different times and places.

Contents

The basics

Things to see & do

Shop 'til you drop

Trips out of Athens

Greece: the lowdown

Internet links

This guide has all the information you need for an enjoyable time tour of Ancient Greece. But if you want to do some more exploring, you can visit the Usborne Quicklinks Website, where you'll find links to fantastic websites. Just go to www.usborne-quicklinks.com and enter the keywords "guide to ancient greece".

Before using the internet, please read the internet safety guidelines on the Usborne Quicklinks Website.

A note on dates

If you see "BC" after a date, it means "Before Christ" - his birth, that is, which was about 2,000 years ago. So 449BC is 449 years before the birth of Christ - about 2,449 years ago. Some dates have "c." in front. It stands for *circa*, which means "about" in Latin.

Part one
The basics

Picture Greece... sandy beaches lapped by the sparkling Mediterranean Sea. Perfect if you want to sit around making sand castles and paddling all day.

Now forget all that. If you're looking for a real adventure, join me on a trip back in time, over 2,000 years ago, to Ancient Greece. If it's your first visit, or even if it's your first trip back in time, DON'T PANIC! I'll be with you all the way, filling you in on everything a time tourist needs to know.

This tourist is all set to explore Ancient Greece. With the help of this guide, you will be too.

Ancient Greece

The area shaded in green is the land the Greeks colonized nearly 2,500 years ago – the time when you'll be visiting.

Macedonia

Thrace

Zeus, king of the gods, feeling grumpy

Mount Olympus
Home of the gods when they're not out causing trouble elsewhere

Thessaly

Chalcidice

Aegean Sea

Troy
Site of a legendary Greek victory, involving the army and a large wooden horse

Lesbos

N

Kos
The island where Hippocrates has set up his medical school.

Delos
History-loving island-hoppers should stop off here where the Delian League (an alliance of Greek states) met for the first time.

A trireme (Greek warship)

Unlike merchant ships, triremes have oars as well as sails.

Mediterranean Sea

Enormous statue of Athene

Laurion
Site of the ancient world's largest silver mines

This way to Crete – island home of the fabled Minotaur

Athens
The city-state with everything, including an enormous statue of Athene

Attica

Mycenae

Argos

Sparta
Home of the scary Spartans: for info only. DON'T visit! They don't like tourists – or anyone else come to that

Piraeus
Port of Athens and home to traders from everywhere

Arcadia

Messenia

Peloponnese

A Spartan warrior keeping his slave hard at it

Delphi
Home of the famous oracle, who can answer any question you care to ask

The Pythia (oracle at Delphi) having a vision

Olympia
See the original Olympics here.

Merchants on the way to Sicily dump an unwanted passenger.

Ancient where?

All Greek to me

A quick word of warning. Confusingly, the Ancient Greeks never called themselves Greeks. As far as they were concerned, they were "Hellenes", and the land they lived in was "Hellas".

In fact, it was the Ancient Romans who first called the Hellenes "Graeci" when they conquered the place in the 2nd century BC.

When you visit, stick to "Hellenes". That way people won't think you're crazy.

Perhaps you're wondering what the big deal is with Ancient Greece anyway - why not Ancient Spain, or Ancient Bulgaria?

The fact is, the Ancient Greeks were a pretty special bunch. They built incredible buildings, sculpted amazing sculptures, and thought astonishing thoughts, long before anyone else in Europe. Trust me - I've been there.

To get you up to speed on how it all happened, here's a quick rundown of Ancient Greece through the ages, from the earliest settlers to the peak of civilization.

This is me on my last trip to Ancient Greece, cunningly disguised as a local.

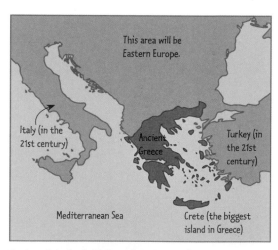

This area will be Eastern Europe.

Italy (in the 21st century)

Ancient Greece

Turkey (in the 21st century)

Mediterranean Sea

Crete (the biggest island in Greece)

The land of the Greeks lies in southern Europe. It's very mountainous, with lots of small islands, and is surrounded by the Mediterranean Sea.

Early Greece

The very first people in Greece lived about 40,000 years ago, but they were too busy hunting and looking for food to be civilized. Don't bother visiting then – there's not much to see, and you might end up dead.

No, it's not a skirt... This young Minoan man is kitted out in a very trendy kilt.

By 2000BC, some people known as the Minoans had built up a civilization on the island of Crete. Meanwhile, another lot, called the Mycenaeans, became top dogs on the mainland. They lorded it over everyone until about 1100BC. Then...

...nobody really knows. The Dark Ages hit. It's called that because people in the 21st century are mostly in the dark about what was happening. There probably weren't any firebreathing monsters, but you never know. My advice is to steer clear.

Even when they were dead, Mycenaean kings were covered in riches – like this golden death mask.

Civilized at last

300 years on, the land was divided into independent "city-states" (each one known as a *polis*), and around 500BC, the Classical Period dawned. This is the time to visit. It only lasted 200 years, so take care timing your trip. If you end up in the Dark Ages, not even this guidebook can help you.

Nudity is popular in Classical Greece – and not just among the statues.

Man with a plan

Look out for Pericles, top dog in Athens from 443–429BC. Pericles isn't your average Athenian politician. On the contrary, he's wise, eloquent and honest.

You'll have to wade through crowds of admirers to get a good glimpse of him.

'Island-hopping' isn't this easy. You'll need a boat.

Planning a trip

Number one on your must-see list: Athens! It's the leading city-state in Ancient Greece, and everyone who is anyone is there.

Come between 479 and 431BC, and you'll be rubbing shoulders with the cream of dramatists, philosophers and sculptors.

First things first

If this is your first experience of time tourism, you'll need to plan things carefully. You can't just grab your swimming costume and a pair of sunglasses and bung them in a suitcase.

First, the good news: you won't need a visa or a passport, and there's no boring paperwork to fill in. The Ancient Greeks welcome foreign visitors - as long as you don't outstay that welcome. After a month, you'll have to start paying taxes. This would be a good time to leave.

But when to visit? If you're planning on lots of sightseeing, go in late spring, when it's warm, but not too hot. Summer can be scorching. Don't go in winter - it's wet and miserable.

10

What to pack

Bed: Bring a light tent and a sleeping bag if you've got them – just in case. There are places to stay (find out more on pages 18-21), but you can't ring up in advance to book a room. There are no telephones, in case you were wondering.

Pack light, like this seasoned tourist. If you were planning to bring five suitcases... forget it.

Food and drink: Bring some food for emergencies. A water bottle is a must. There are wells and fountains to fill up in, but no drinks machines.

Clothes: Take it from me, it's not sensible to wander around Ancient Greece in jeans and trainers. You'll need to buy a tunic from a market on arrival. To protect against the sun and dust, you'll find a wide-brimmed hat and a riding cloak (a *chlamys*) are perfect. You might think you look ridiculous, but the locals won't bat an eyelid.

Currency: You won't be able to get hold of any Ancient Greek money in advance, unless you break into a museum (don't). But if you bring a good supply of spices, you'll be able to trade them for coins when you arrive. Spices are rare in Ancient Greece, which makes them very valuable.

Greek alphabet

Ancient Greek can be tricky to learn, but in case you're planning to take a crash course, here's the alphabet.

Some bits might look familiar. That's because our alphabet comes from the Greek one.

Aα = A	Iι = I	Pρ = R
Bβ = B	Kκ = K	Σσ = S
Γγ = G	Λλ = L	Tτ = T
Δδ = D	M = M	Yυ = U
Eε = E	Nν = N	Φφ = ph
Zζ = Z	Ξξ = X	Xχ = ch
Hη = E	Oo = O	Ψψ = ph
θθ = t	Ππ = P	Ωω = O

11

People use oil instead of soap, then scrape it off with a tool called a strigil.

I've put this symbol next to activities which are male-only, so you don't get caught out.

Dos & don'ts

You'll get in no end of trouble if people start to suspect you're from the 21st century. So, whatever you do, remember the most important rule of time tourism: Always Blend In.

If you think your grandparents are old-fashioned, you haven't seen anything yet. Pay close attention to these tips. They won't just spare your blushes; they could save you from arrest - or worse.

Cleanliness: The Greeks don't have power showers, but they do have a thing about keeping clean. Smell, and your name will be mud. Fortunately, most houses have a bathtub, which you can ask a slave to fill up for you.

His 'n' hers: Sadly, Ancient Greece can be a little unwelcoming if you're a female time tourist. The men are in charge (in public at least), and gender discrimination is a fact of life.

Don't be put off though. There's still plenty to see and do if you're unmarried (wives are usually stuck at home). And if the worst comes to the worst, you could always dress up as a boy.

Seaside scares: Ancient Greece doesn't have any scorpions or lions wandering around (if you're a fan of dangerous animals, try Ancient Egypt instead). But, all the same, there are a few things to watch out for.

If you take a dip in the sea, look out for jellyfish and sea urchins. I like to pack some baking soda and a sewing kit. The baking soda is good for stings, and if you sterilize a needle by holding it over a flame, you can use it to remove the stings of sea urchins.

This sort of thing can look very funny, until it happens to you.

Last but not least: As you read this guide, look out for my handy "Top tips for tourists" like the one on the right. They're little things I've discovered in the course of my own travels, and they'll help you get the most out of your stay (and steer clear of embarrassing blunders).

That's it. Now it's time to pack your bag, and travel back in time...

Touch of the sun?

This might be the ancient world, but just as in the 21st century, nothing says "tourist" more clearly than a sunburn.

Don't forget to pack your sun cream, and always cover up if you're going outside.

Top tips for tourists

No. 1: Persian pests

When chatting to locals, don't mention the Persians. They invaded Greece in 480BC, destroyed lots of temples, and were only thrown out a year later. It's a touchy subject.

On the other hand, if you visit after 448BC, the Greeks will have crushed the Persians in a series of epic battles, which you'll soon get sick of hearing about.

Athens

Welcome to Greece! It's more than 2,000 years before you were (sorry, will be) born. I hope you had a pleasant journey.

First stop, Athens – the number one city-state in Greece. This picture shows the heart of the city, to help you get your bearings.

A bird's eye view of the heart of Athens

The Panathenaic Way

These covered shops are called *stoae*.

This is the Agora, where everyone comes for groceries and gossip.

Slave auctions take place here. Watch you don't scratch your nose and accidentally make a bid.

This way to the Dipylon Gate, one of the city's main entrances.

This is the main road from the city to the Acropolis, and it's called the Panathenaic Way. It's used during the Panathenean Festival (see page 43).

You'll soon notice that the city skyline is dominated by a rocky hill topped with temples. This is called the Acropolis (meaning "top of the city"). To get a real feel for the city, head here as soon as you arrive.

The Tholos, where council leaders meet

The Bouleuterion, where the city council hold their meetings

Most Athenian craftsmen live and work over here.

This elegant temple is dedicated to Hephaestos, god of craftsmen. (Locals call it the Theseum.)

What not to wear

Take a good look at this picture so you know what NOT to wear on the Acropolis.

This man is dressed as a Persian warrior – not a good look in Athens. No Greek would be seen dead in such outlandish clothing.

The Acropolis

This is where the Athenians first settled, and now it's the holiest site in the city, not to mention the most important place in Greece... if you ask the Athenians, that is.

But as proud as the citizens are of their sacred Acropolis, remember it was only recently, in 480BC, that the Persians fought their way into the city and trashed the whole hilltop.

To see the Acropolis at its best, visit after 468BC. That year saw the Battle of Eurymedon, when the Greeks smashed the Persians on land and at sea. Pericles, hero of the hour, will be doing up the Acropolis to prove that Athens is number one.

Don't get me started on the Parthenon... Let's just say it's stunning, the most beautiful temple in Greece.

The Acropolis

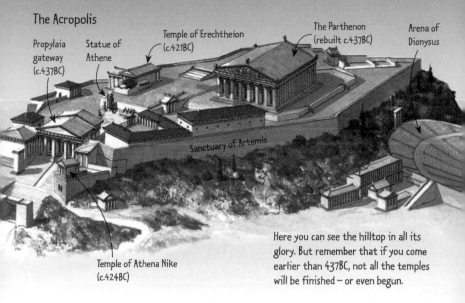

Propylaia gateway (c.437BC)

Statue of Athene

Temple of Erechtheion (c.421BC)

The Parthenon (rebuilt c.437BC)

Arena of Dionysus

Sanctuary of Artemis

Temple of Athena Nike (c.424BC)

Here you can see the hilltop in all its glory. But remember that if you come earlier than 437BC, not all the temples will be finished – or even begun.

Exploring the hilltop

Go through the lavish Propylaia gateway, and you'll be face to face with a giant statue of Athene, the patron goddess of the city. And by "giant" I mean it's so big, it can be seen from well out at sea. Athene's sister Artemis gets a look-in too, although she only gets a small sanctuary.

The biggest draw for tourists is the Parthenon, a temple dedicated to Athene (read about it on page 40). On the other side of the hill is the Arena of Dionysus, god of wine and drama, which is where plays are performed.

Top tips for tourists

No. 2: A holy horde

You might be getting confused by all this talk of gods and goddesses. The Greeks worship so many of them it's hard to keep count.

For a holy who's who, have a look at my guide to the most important gods and goddesses – you'll find it on pages 100–103.

You can usually tell if you've got a chance of getting in. This tourist should try elsewhere.

Where to stay

You'll soon be needing a bed for the night. Ancient Greeks visiting Athens will usually stay with friends or relatives, but that's not an option for you unless you speak the language, and make friends quickly. Or unless you've traced your ancestors all the way back to Ancient Greece. But, even then, they might not believe you.

Personally, I enjoy camping out. The weather's warm for most of the year, and lots of people sleep under porches in the Agora. With so many people in the same place, it's also safe... Well, safe-ish.

Hotels

If camping isn't your cup of tea, don't worry. Large towns have smart hotels, called *katagogia*. They're pricey, but it's worth trying to check into one, just for the experience.

Unfortunately, many *katagogia* are exclusive. They cater for VIPs, and I'm afraid that doesn't include you. So you'll have to be very persuasive if you plan on talking your way in.

18

House guest

There's one other possibility – you may be able to rent rooms in a private house. If you get to stay in a house as big as the one below, you've struck gold. Most are much smaller, though the rooms are similar.

Well-to-do Greek houses are often built around a central courtyard that's a bit like a garden, with the rooms facing in. People here like their privacy.

Key

1. Slaves' room
2. Bathroom
3. Lobby
4. Bedroom for rent
5. Altar for the household god
6. Well
7. A potter's workshop
8. The *andron*: men only!
9. Kitchen
10. Women's quarters

Normally the roof goes all the way round the house. But this way, you can see the rooms inside...

Slaving over a hot stove

Guests waiting in the lobby

A herm: statue of the god Hermes to protect the house

House rules

If you can wangle a room in a rich citizen's house, you'll have a very comfortable stay. Some houses even have a bakery on the ground floor, so breakfast will be a piece of cake (well, bread actually).

There aren't many house rules, but here's one you mustn't forget: if you're a male tourist, NEVER go near the women's quarters without being invited. If you do, the landlord might think you're trying to run away with his wife or daughter, and he won't be very happy.

Put your feet up

In the richest households, the furniture is stunning - beautifully carved and inlaid with ivory, gold and silver - not to mention, surprisingly comfortable.

The master of the house gets the best seat. Here he is relaxing on his *thronos*.

A word of warning, though. There'll be one chair that's a lot fancier than the others. Don't sit in it - it's for the master of the house. The Greeks call this chair a *thronos* (that's where we get the word "throne" from). Other men have to make do with stools. For once, women get a better deal - they can sit on chairs.

20

Lighten up

The good news is you won't face a big electricity bill at the end of your stay. The bad news? You guessed it - there's no electricity. People rely on oil lamps, so rooms can get very dim after dark.

That lovely soft glow makes for some cosy evenings, though. Don't be tempted to bring a torch. If you're caught using one, people will probably think you're a magician - fun for a bit, until they start asking you to make money appear out of thin air.

These oil lamp stands are popular because they're so stylish and practical.

Take a look around

In many rooms the walls are decorated with brightly patterned tapestries, made by the women of the house. After all, they have to do something while they're stuck at home all day. If you want to get in your host's good books, try some admiring comments about the wall hangings - they were probably made by his wife.

There are no fitted carpets in ancient Greek houses, but there are usually some very fine mosaics - patterns and pictures made up of tiny stones in different shades, set into the floor.

Don't get distracted gazing down at the pretty mosaics. You might walk into someone.

This painting from a pot shows a happy hunter heading home, heaving his hefty haul – a fox and a hare.

Top tips for tourists

No. 4: Catch of the day

Seafood fans are in for a treat. You're never too far from the coast, and the seas are brimming with a wide variety of tasty sea creatures.

I recommend kalamari (squid) – it's popular with the locals, and delicious as long as it's cooked properly. Otherwise it can be more rubbery than an eraser.

What to eat

Don't worry, you won't have to eat pigs' snouts or sautéed mice - this isn't Ancient Rome. The Greeks prefer to keep it simple. Wherever you go, you'll find a generous supply of bread, cheese, eggs, fish, fruit and vegetables. The locals also eat lots of barley porridge. It's cheap and nutritious, although not exactly a taste sensation.

Meat is expensive. If you can't live without it, you'll need to pack extra supplies of spices to trade with. There's lamb, pork and poultry for those who can afford it, plus goat, which is more of an acquired taste. There aren't many cows (the land is too mountainous for them to graze), so a nice steak will cost you an arm and a leg.

The main meal

Have you ever heard it said that you should, "Breakfast like a king, dine like a pauper"? Well, for the Greeks it's the other way round (except for the poor, who eat like paupers all the time).

Breakfast is usually just a piece of bread soaked in wine, lunch is a light snack, and dinner is a real feast.

Cheers!

The Greeks are very fond of wine. They dilute it with water in vast containers, called *kraters*. Diluting is important. The wine is strong, and no respectable Greek would dream of drinking it on its own. I'd steer well clear if I were you - you're better off drinking water at a public fountain.

Kraters can be huge. Some are as big as a large dog.

Olive oil

Olives or their oil turn up in almost every Greek dish. In fact, Homer, the most famous Ancient Greek poet, was so enthusiastic about olive oil that he called it "liquid gold". You might not feel quite so strongly, but you're sure to eat a lot of it.

The Greeks are so potty about olives that they even decorate vases with olive-picking scenes. This vase is an *amphora*. It's slightly smaller than a *krater*.

Olives are pressed several times over, and each pressing gives a different grade of oil. Each grade has its own use - from medicine to fuel, and even an Ancient Greek version of sun cream (you'll get used to it). The best grade, which is used for cooking and eating, comes from the first pressing.

If you're in the countryside, look out for olive presses like this one. Olives are put inside and squashed to get the oil out.

23

This is a Greek drinking cup, called a *kylix*. It's very wide and shallow, so try not to spill the contents all over your host's couch.

Forget the food – even the dinner plates look good enough to eat.

❝ *In some parts they call a sumptuous banquet. "having a bite to eat".* **❞**

Socrates, a philosopher, amazed at the extravagance of the richest Greeks

Out for dinner ♂

A Greek dinner party is fun for all the family. Well, actually just for the men, as wives and children are strictly Not Invited. Even the host's family has to eat in a separate room.

If you're a male time tourist, you're likely to get plenty of invitations, and it's well worth accepting one or two.

Dinnertime

You won't get in trouble for slumping at the dinner table. Everyone reclines on cushions (you can even bring your own), and eats from small tables within easy reach. The host will have made a seating plan (well, a reclining plan), so you'll be told where to go. If you're on his right, congratulations! You're the most important guest.

Bring your appetite: there are a lot of dishes. There'll be fish, meat and vegetables, cheeses, nuts and fruit, all set out on small tables within easy reach of your couch. But it's only when the food is finished that the evening really gets going. That's when the drinking and debating begins (find out more on pages 34-35).

If you arrive late, the best seats may have gone.

Guests listen to live music while they eat.

The food is brought in, already laid out on tables.

Just wave a hand to have your cup refilled.

Male diners are entertained by the witty chat of professional female companions.

Party etiquette

There are a few things to remember. First, dress smartly and arrive on time - the other diners won't wait. It's fine to eat with your fingers (there are no forks), but spoons are available. Instead of napkins, guests wipe their hands on a special cleansing paste. Don't eat it. It tastes revolting, and the other guests will enjoy telling the one about the clueless foreigner for months to come.

Putting your foot in it

When you arrive, the host's slaves will rinse and perfume your feet. If you've spent all day on foot, they'll be grateful if you've washed them first.

25

Getting around

Greece's spectacular mountains make for great views, but they're not such fun when it comes to travel. The endless ups and downs make any journey hard going. It's such a slog to get anywhere that most Greeks just don't bother (unless it's a trip to the local temple to keep the gods happy).

Luckily, the busiest routes have pretty decent roads. There aren't many bridges, so if you need to cross a river go in summer, when water levels are low.

A horse-drawn cart can seem like the answer to all your travel problems... until you get stuck in the mud.

Carting the load

Cars won't be available for a VERY long time, so if you need a vehicle, it's a choice between a cart (slow and steady) or a chariot (fast and flashy). Both are expensive, and if anything goes wrong you won't be able to call a breakdown service.

My advice is to make like the locals, and walk. You'll have to lug your backpack around, but you could always hire a mule to take the weight. It's nice to have a bit of company, even if the conversation isn't very stimulating.

If you go for a horse, you won't get saddle sore. There are no saddles.

Travel warning

The Greeks love fighting each other, so make sure your route doesn't take you through a battlefield. Nothing ruins a nice spot of hiking like getting stuck in a battle or being arrested as a spy.

Avoid war zones, unless you're sure you can talk your way out of a tight spot.

It gets worse: many areas, especially in the highlands, are overrun with bandits. So always check if you're in a dangerous area - you might prefer to stay put. Or at least join up with a group of locals going in the same direction.

Walking gear

Most Greek walkers won't go anywhere without a walking stick and folding stool. Don't laugh. You'll soon follow their example.

The stick helps on the rough ground and the stool is great for a rest after climbing a hill.

Two other essentials: water, and a torch (of the flaming variety – pack some matches). It might be a pain to carry, but you'll thank me when darkness falls.

Keep your eyes peeled – bandits are fond of sneaking up on their victims and catching them unawares.

27

A Sea voyage

❝ ...in order to cheat their creditors, they laid a plot to sink (the ship).❞

Demosthenes, a great speechmaker, with a reminder not to get stuck on a ship with the wrong crowd

Overall, land travel is slow, dull and potentially fatal. It's more sensible to make journeys by sea - though perhaps not that much more sensible, as you'll see.

Most boats have sails and oars, and can be pretty speedy if the wind is good. You're sure to find a merchant ship to take you - for a price, of course. The downside? Be careful whose ship you travel on. A crew can turn on the passengers and rob them at sea, where there's no one to stop them.

A merchant ship to avoid: its crew looks distinctly unfriendly

There are stories of hapless passengers being thrown overboard and rescued by dolphins. But you can't trust stories – or dolphins.

Even if your crew doesn't turn on you, it's not all plain sailing. There are threats from storms, hidden rocks and pirates. At least you're visiting at a time when the Athenian navy is at its most powerful. They watch over the seas, so the risk of attack is fairly low.

You might spot one of these onboard your vessel. It's not a weapon – it's an anchor. The spikes hold it in the sea bed.

These pirates are bound to come to a sticky end.

Sail safe

If you're making a sea voyage, do it in summer to avoid storms, but when there's a decent wind. So long as you trust the captain, you should be alright. A good test is to check whether he's made a sacrifice to the sea god Poseidon before setting sail. It might not help, but at least it shows he takes his responsibility seriously.

Top tips for tourists

No. 5: Travel inn blues

Whether you travel by land or by sea, you'll have difficulty finding an inn for the night.

Luckily for the tourist, most Greeks see it as their duty to look after people on long journeys out of town.

If you need a place to stay, you can knock on almost any door and expect a warm welcome. Always repay your hosts with gifts from home – and don't stay long.

If you get sick...

...you're in the right place. Greek doctors have an excellent reputation. That doesn't mean all of them are excellent though. Read these pages carefully before trusting your health to any old fraudster offering a miracle cure. There are plenty of them. (Fraudsters, that is, not miracle cures.)

Priests and prayers

Most Greeks keep herbal medicines for minor illnesses. But for anything more serious, they'll call in a priest (they double up as doctors). He'll offer home-made remedies – if you dare take them.

He might also suggest staying overnight in one of the temples of Asclepius, god of healing. It's worth a shot. This "treatment" can produce miraculous results, if the stories are to be believed...

You'll have to perform sacrifices before you can spend a night in the temple. This can mean anything from killing animals to offering honey cakes (hope for the latter). Asclepius might heal you as you sleep, or tell you in a dream what treatment you need. Or, you'll wake up feeling no better.

Some patients who stay in a temple dream Asclepius is healing them, and wake up right as rain. Or so they say.

30

A thank-you gift

If Asclepius does help, you'll need to leave him an offering to say thank you. I'm afraid a bunch of flowers won't do. Strangely, Asclepius seems to like getting a model of the body part he's cured. Fine if you had a sore foot, but a bit awkward if your problem was in a more embarrassing area.

This lucky patient had his leg cured by Asclepius.

The new science

My advice? Forget priests and find a doctor who follows the new "Hippocratic" method. Hippocrates has founded a medical school on the island of Kos. He teaches his students to ask questions and examine patients to find out what the problem is – just like 21st century doctors.

Hippocrates' students take anatomy lessons, often cutting up dead bodies. So they have some sort of idea what goes on under your skin.

The Hippocratic method is based on the shocking notion that illness isn't actually a punishment from the gods. But even these doctors have a healthy respect for Asclepius. It'll be a long time before their patients get used to the idea that they can be cured without help from the gods.

If you need an operation, it's time to head home. There are no antiseptics and no painkillers.

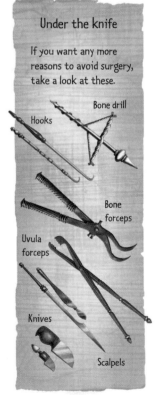

Under the knife

If you want any more reasons to avoid surgery, take a look at these.

Hooks

Bone drill

Bone forceps

Uvula forceps

Knives

Scalpels

The cure

The bad news? Even if a Hippocratic doctor works out what's wrong, the chances are he won't do very much. Hippocrates believes most ailments clear up on their own, so the "cure" will probably just be lots of rest, combined with a healthy diet.

It could be worse, though. Some medical men think disease is carried in the blood, and the obvious solution is to bleed the patient until they're well again – or dead. If an enthusiastic doctor offers to open a vein for you, make your excuses and get out. And if he suggests surgery... flee.

Pay up!

As long as you've got a big dose of spices to pay with, you can be sure of the doctor of your choice. You can also be sure of attracting one or two con artists, so make sure you get the real thing.

Even if you don't have a bean (or, more usefully, a peppercorn), you'll still be able to get medical treatment. Most city-states pay doctors so that poor people can be treated free of charge.

Part two
Things to see & do

So now you know enough to survive in Ancient Greece. But what is there to do?

Well, for starters, there's more culture than you can shake a spear at. In fact, your only problem is choosing where to start - whether it's enjoying the incredible art and music, taking part in the biggest festivals or watching the latest plays.

If you're lucky, you'll even get to gossip at the finest dinner parties or, best of all, catch a nugget of knowledge from world-class thinkers - the philosophers.

Ancient Greek musicians strike up a tune.

Hetairai, like this one from a vase painting, are the only women allowed to say anything at a symposium.

Top tips for tourists

No. 6: Riddle-me-ree

One popular symposium game is asking riddles, with forfeits (like drinking some salty water) if you get the answer wrong. Have a go at this one:

Don't speak and you'll express my name; say my name and you won't express me at all!

Give up?

The answer is "silence".

Talk the talk ♂

There's nothing Ancient Greek men love better than the sound of their own voices. Between you and me, most of them could talk the hind legs off several donkeys.

You don't need to look far to see the evidence. At any dinner party, it's not the food the guests are looking forward to, but the symposium. This is a very long after-dinner debate on any topic you can think of (and a few more besides). Once again it's men only, though many female time tourists will be relieved to miss out.

The only women present are hired companions called *hetairai* - professional party girls who are pretty, young and witty.

Master of ceremonies

Before the symposium gets going, the men choose a *symposiarch*, who's usually the host or the most important guest. He's in charge of how strong the wine will be.

If the *symposiarch* is in the mood for a good discussion, he'll order the slaves to water it down a lot. If he orders it to be left strong, the chances are the conversation won't be so serious.

Party games

If you're thinking that several hours of debate doesn't sound like a barrel of laughs, don't worry - it isn't all talk. There's also music, dancing, acrobatics and - best of all - the much-loved game, *kottabos*.

Anyone who's played darts before will have a head start in this game. The four steps are shown below. It's important to get it right first time, because the worse a player is, the more they have to drink - and the worse they become...

1. Finish all the drink, except the last mouthful.

2. Swirl the dregs around the bowl.

3. Hurl the contents at a target.

4. Miss, and you get your bowl refilled.

35

Public speaking

If you want to hear some really first-class public speaking, a symposium might not be for you.

Instead, go to see a trial. With no lawyers, citizens have to defend themselves – though the sensible ones pay a professional writer to write a speech for them. Thankfully all speeches are timed, so people don't ramble on forever.

The verdict is debated by a jury, several hundred strong and all male (surprise, surprise). With such a huge jury, no one can afford to bribe the whole lot.

Time's up!

Speeches are timed with a water clock. When all the water from the top pot has run into the pot below, time is up. Keep an eye on it though. Shadier citizens try to increase their time by weeing in the top pot when no one is looking.

Getting philosophical

Even better than a trial is a trip to a market place, where philosophers attract large crowds. Philosopher means "lover of knowledge" in Ancient Greek.

But they're mostly interested in the purpose of the universe and the meaning of life, which is quite enough to keep them going.

Each member of the jury puts one of these tokens in a pot to vote.

Tokens with a hollow middle mean "guilty".

Tokens with a solid middle mean "innocent".

A guide to philosophers

Socrates

Socrates: the father of philosophy himself. You may think of Socrates as an old man with a beard, but right now, he's about 35 - see him now, before he gets really famous. Just look out for the ugly one discussing truth, good and evil.

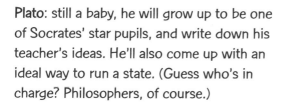

Plato

Plato: still a baby, he will grow up to be one of Socrates' star pupils, and write down his teacher's ideas. He'll also come up with an ideal way to run a state. (Guess who's in charge? Philosophers, of course.)

Aristotle

Aristotle: a pupil of Plato, he won't be born until after your visit. He'll be very keen on politics and science, and will teach Alexander the Great (a Macedonian king who'll conquer most of the known world).

The Stoics: a group of philosophers named after the *stoa* (porch) where they meet to agree with each other. They think people should lead a calm life.

Diogenes

Diogenes: founder of the group known as **Cynics**, who don't believe in rules and dislike too much wealth. At least Diogenes lives by his beliefs - he's recently moved into a large barrel.

Even gods sometimes behave badly. This vase painting shows Zeus, disguised as an eagle, pouncing on an unsuspecting woman.

Top temples

Fancy nosing round the home of a god? If so, a visit to a temple might be just what you need.

Let me explain... The Greeks think the gods are pretty much the same as humans, only a lot more powerful. So temples aren't just places to worship, they're places for the gods to live (luxury apartments, if you like). People usually pray at home, only heading to the temples for festivals. A god doesn't want hundreds of people tramping in and out of his home every day.

Rites & wrongs

For the full temple experience, you might like to enter into the spirit of it all and pray. Whatever problem you have, the Greeks are sure to have a god who can help you out. Look at pages 100-103 if you're not sure which one.

You'll need to take a gift, and it had better be a good one – gods are fussy. If you're stuck, ask a priest, who'll be happy to help. Being a priest is just like any other job. At work, they're holy; at home, they're like everyone else.

A tiny, charred offering won't go down well. You might meet with an "accident".

Bigger & better

Most temples are fully fledged divine mansions (short on rooms, but nicely decorated). But it wasn't always like this. It's only in the last few hundred years that architects have started building really magnificent homes for the gods.

The first temples were no more than a *cella* (a room) with a porch and pillar entrance. The *cella* housed a statue, but that was it.

Later, more elaborate temples were built, with a porch at the back as well as at the front.

Finally, designers introduced the *peristyle* – a porch running all the way round (if eight pillars are good, 34 must be better).

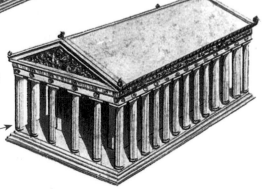

The Parthenon

Top tips for tourists

No. 8: Fabulous frieze

It's a tiring climb up to the Parthenon, so catch your breath by admiring the frieze that decorates the outside of the temple. It shows dramatic scenes from legend, including strange creatures called centaurs (they're half-man, half-horse, and don't really exist).

High up on the Acropolis, there's one temple that's literally head and shoulders above the rest: the Parthenon. Dedicated to Athene, it's the star attraction of the Acropolis, not to mention Athens, and probably the whole of Ancient Greece. A visit here is a must.

The exterior is fabulous, but wait until you get inside. Here something even more impressive awaits - a gigantic statue of "Athene Parthenos" (Athene the maiden), lovingly created by the master sculptor Pheidias. It's this stunning statue that gives the temple its name.

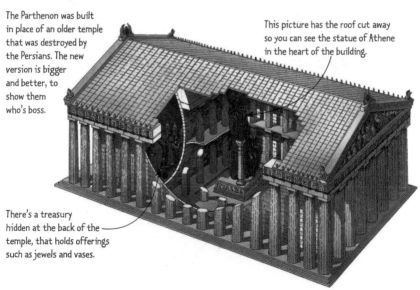

The Parthenon was built in place of an older temple that was destroyed by the Persians. The new version is bigger and better, to show them who's boss.

This picture has the roof cut away so you can see the statue of Athene in the heart of the building.

There's a treasury hidden at the back of the temple, that holds offerings such as jewels and vases.

A closer look at Athene's statue

The statue is said to have cost more than the entire temple – up close, you'll see why.

In her right hand Athene holds a statuette of Nike, goddess of victory.

The headpiece displays the Sphinx, a legendary monster.

66 Athene leaped from her father's head and shouted aloud... 99

The poet Pindar describing Athene's unusual birth

The statue stands 12m (40ft) high. You'd need binoculars to see her face properly (but you'd get some pretty funny looks).

The statue is made out of wood, but it's covered in ivory for the skin, and beaten gold for the dress.

Athene rests her left hand on a shield supported by a serpent. This is a symbol of Erechtheus, her adopted son and early ruler of Athens.

41

Ancient Greek "Trick or Treating" – children go from door to door for fruit and cakes. Instead of dressing up, they carry poles wound with wool.

Fabulous festivals

The Greeks don't get a break at weekends, but to make up for it they have plenty of festivals. They're like giant parties for the gods - though of course it's really the humans who enjoy the music, drama, sport and food on offer. It's easy to get carried away and forget the point, which is to persuade the gods to listen to prayers.

God vs. goddess

In Athens, most festivals finish up at the temples on the Acropolis. It's the holiest place in the city, and not just because it's crammed with temples. According to legend, it's here that Athene and Poseidon (the god of the ocean) fought over which of them should be the patron god(dess) of Athens.

Poseidon offered the citizens vast wealth through trade over the seas, while Athene simply planted an olive tree. But the citizens obviously thought the tree was a better deal, because Athene was declared the winner and the city was named after her. You can see the tree on the Acropolis, in the courtyard of the Erechtheion Temple.

Poseidon fights Athene. (Guess who won.)

42

Best of the fests

If you're in Athens in the summer, look out for the Panathenea, held each year for Athene. Every four years it becomes the Great Panathenea and lasts for six days. Everyone gets dressed up in their best clothes, and even Athene gets a fashionable new frock (well, her statue does). The highlight is a grand procession to the Acropolis.

A golden dress is carried by boat to Athene's statue on the Acropolis.

The procession of Panathenea

Dancers, musicians, soldiers and priests all process along the Panathenaic Way.

Important citizens lead the parade, followed by the offering bearers.

The Panathenea procession leaves from the Dipylon Gate: just follow the crowds.

Top tips for tourists

No. 9: Cow to go

Want a free meal? Join the procession to a temple. Cattle are sacrificed, cooked, and the meat is handed out to festival-goers.

An actor "corpsing"

Dramatic arts

Plays are all the rage in Athens, and the best of the bunch are the tragedies. With grand themes (murder, conflict, blood all over the dinner table), they could turn into real gore-fests.

But don't worry if you're squeamish. All the violence happens offstage, with a narrator telling you what's going on. The odd "dead" body is carted on, but that's it.

A buffoon in a comedy

Light relief

If you don't fancy all that doom and gloom, try a comedy. It'll be very silly with plenty of rude jokes, a bit like a pantomime. The only downside is that a lot of the fun is at the expense of stars and politicians of the day, so you'll have to read up on current affairs first.

A man playing a satyr in a tragi-comedy – or is it a comi-tragedy?

There are also satyr plays, which are the weirdest of the lot. They're comedies which poke fun at tragedies. The name comes from some of the cast who dress up as satyrs: half-men, half-beasts. It can be very confusing if you're not used to it.

44

The Dionysia

Hardcore drama addicts should visit Athens during the Dionysia. Named after Dionysus (the god of both wine and drama), it's a week-long religious and drama fest.

After the first day's processions and sacrifices come the drama competitions. Each year, three tragedy and five comedy writers - the crème de la crème - make the shortlist. You may well see a play which will still be performed 2,500 years later.

Birth of the play

If you need any more reason to go, consider this: the Ancient Greeks practically invented plays. It all began with the Dionysia, which started as a countryside festival. A group of 50 singing, masked dancers, called the chorus, used to act out legends, reciting lines together. Over time, the chorus got smaller, and three actors began taking solos, sharing up to 45 parts.

When you visit, the dialogue between soloists is the most important part, and the chorus just passes the odd comment and links events together. All of the actors are male - even the ones playing women.

Chorus leader

Plays can be expensive to put on, so during the Dionysia, each one is funded by a rich citizen, known as a *choregos*, or chorus leader.

Choregoi like to compete with each other, buying the most expensive props and costumes they can, to show off how rich and generous they are.

It sounds crazy, but it can be worth it. If his play is a hit, a *choregos* is adored by his fellow citizens.

A tragic actor launches into an emotional speech. You could be here for hours.

45

The "modern" stage

Reserved!

Sit on one of these chairs instead of the stone benches, and you'll get thrown out. They're for VIPs, such as foreign diplomats and competition judges.

The first plays ever to be shown in Athens were in the marketplace, with the audience sitting in makeshift wooden stands. Then one year there was a disaster: the stands collapsed, killing several people. After that, the Athenians learnt their lesson and built a permanent, open-air arena out of stone.

Drama is now so popular that you'll be able to watch plays in a stone arena in any big city in the Greek world.

An open-air arena

The actors change in here.

Altar

Arenas are gigantic, holding up to 18,000 spectators.

Chorus members chant, sing and dance in the orchestra (that's a dancing floor, not a group of musicians).

Setting the scene

There's just one snag. In big arenas, the actors are about as easy to spot as performing fleas. So their costumes have to show clearly who's who. It's pretty simple: happy characters dress brightly, and tragic ones wear dark clothes. The actors are also lumbered with masks, wigs and platform boots. Try not to laugh, especially if you're watching a tragedy.

Actors' masks are made of stiffened fabric or cork, and then painted.

The masks have very exaggerated expressions so the audience can see them from a distance.

Special effects

The gods make guest appearances in some plays. A special crane lifts up the actor playing the god or goddess, so it looks as if they're flying. But as you're used to astonishing special effects in 21st century films, you might find it a bit unconvincing.

Top tips
for tourists

No. 10: Box office

To get in, buy a token for 2 obols. It will have a letter showing which row to sit in (blocks of seats are divided into city districts, and in some arenas, women sit separately from men).

Don't worry if you're stuck at the back. The arenas have fantastic acoustics, so you'll hear every word. Whether you can make out what's going on is another matter.

66 To achieve spectacular effects, the skill of the costume maker is more important than that of the playwright. 99

Aristotle, the philosopher, will be very keen on drama.

Entertainment

All those long dramatic speeches can get a little tedious, so if you're bored of plays (or if you never liked them in the first place), there are lots of other options: from music, poetry and dance to board games.

Young children get their fun too. Toddlers play with dolls, hoops, rattles, tops, and even yoyos (not the flashing plastic kind, though). All the same, parents must keep an eye on their offspring. There are plenty of less suitable toys lying around in Ancient Greece - like swords and spears.

Shakers

Timpanon

Cymbals

Syrinx or panpipes

Auloi

Harp

A horn

Getting into the party spirit

Just like bands in the 21st century, Greek musicians can be very noisy when they get together.

Music & movement

If you've been wondering what ancient Greek songs sound like, you're not alone. The Greeks don't do written music, so no one in the 21st century has ever heard any. Apart from me, of course... But I don't want to spoil your surprise.

At least some of the instruments might be familiar: harps, cymbals and panpipes. But look out for the *auloi* - which is made up of two pipes, played by one man at the same time. That doesn't mean it's twice as good, I'm afraid.

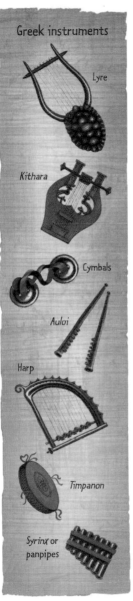

Greek instruments

Lyre

Kithara

Cymbals

Auloi

Harp

Timpanon

Syrinx or panpipes

Dancing is considered one of the highest art forms in Greece.

This painting from a vase shows a rhapsode just getting into his stride.

Rapping rhapsodes

The Greeks adore poetry. It's chanted with a musical backing to add atmosphere - like an ancient version of rapping.

In fact, the men who earn their living reciting poetry are called rhapsodes. They have incredible memories - they know epic poems (each one several books long) by heart. It's very impressive, but can get pretty boring if you don't understand a word of Ancient Greek.

Top tips for tourists

No. 11: Amuse a muse

Every artist needs a bit of inspiration now and then, whether they're a writer, a dancer or a musician. Ancient Greeks believe this comes from nine goddesses called muses, each in charge of a different art form.

If someone persuades you to show off your dancing skills, why not call on a muse for help? It can't hurt.

Goal!

There are less "cultural" pursuits, though. For example, sports fans will be delighted to know that the Greeks play a game that's similar to hockey - but more violent.

Two players face off before a match.

THINGS TO SEE & DO

Just the one

Many Greeks like nothing better than a nice drop of wine. Unfortunately, some of them tend to overdo it a bit. Sensible drinkers follow the advice of the scroll on the right. It's a saying that's currently doing the rounds in Athens.

A wealthy Greek enjoying a cup of wine

❝ *The first cup means health, the second pleasure. The third cup is for sleep... then wise men go home. The fourth cup means rudeness, the fifth shouting. The sixth is disorder... The seventh... black eyes and the eighth brings a police summons.* **❞**

Advice from the poet Eubulus

Blood sports

Sadly, there are some activities in Greece that you'll want to avoid. One of the most popular "sports" is to make animals fight to the death. These can be anything from cockerels to cats or dogs, and some people place bets on which animal will win. If someone invites you to one of these events, simply decline politely.

A night in

If you're fed up with walking around, there are some activities you can enjoy indoors. If you're staying with a Greek family, suggest a game of "Blind Man's Buff" (think "tag" with a blindfold). It's not just for children – the whole family gets involved.

51

Egyptian statue   Greek statue

The first attempts at sculpture, "borrowing" from the Egyptians...

Art & Sculpture

The Greeks love showing off how cultured they are. So, like it or not, you're going to see a lot of art. There are wall paintings, tapestries and vases galore... but it's the sculptures that will knock your socks off.

Early Greek sculptors didn't bother with anything fancy - they just copied Egyptian statues, which were quite stiff and formal. But, by the time you arrive, you'll find stunningly lifelike statues wherever you go.

The body beautiful

You might think that some pictures of models in the 21st century look too good to be true. Well, it's no different here. From their statues, you'd think all Greek women were beautiful goddesses, and all men were hunky athletes - but you'd be wrong.

All the same, the best sculptors have the knack of showing perfectly realistic, perfectly proportioned human figures, so lifelike they could be real people frozen in time.

And as for the clothes draped round their bodies - you may have to touch them to prove to yourself that they're really stone.

...and the new style: elegant and graceful. Not to mention, very realistic.

52

Self-expression

Of course, not everyone can afford to have their statue put up in the streets, so most of the statues you'll see will be of the stars of the day, whether they're politicians or athletes. Sculptors pride themselves on how accurate these likenesses are.

When they're not busy sculpting the great and the good, they do a fine line in gods and goddesses, too. Pheidias is the name on everyone's lips. As well as his statue of Athene on the Acropolis, don't miss his sculpture of Zeus on a throne at Olympia.

The cutting edge

Art buffs might be interested to know that sculptors will eventually get bored of gods and heroes. They'll start doing everyday characters instead, sometimes even ugly ones. That's pretty shocking stuff to an Ancient Greek who's used to seeing "perfect" statues everywhere.

This statue of a boxer was made after your trip. Instead of striking a heroic pose, he's just having a rest.

Top tips
for tourists

No. 12: Statues to go

You might find that you love Greek statues so much, you want to take one home with you.

If so, you could commission a mini statue of your own. Or, if you're on a budget, go for a terracotta figurine.

Production line

66 *With amazing skill, he carved a statue from snow-white ivory, and gave her beauty that no woman of the world could ever equal.* **99**

Ovid, a Roman, tells the tale of the Greek sculptor Pygmalion. He was so good, he fell in love with a statue he'd made.

So how is a sculpture sculpted? First, the material is chosen: usually bronze, limestone or marble. The stone ones are cut roughly into shape at the quarry, and then taken to a workshop.

It's here that sculptors get to work with mallets and chisels, turning lumps of stone into elegant works of art. As long as you don't distract them, they'll let you watch.

All dolled up

You might think of Ancient Greek statues as pristine white, but actually most of them are painted. (By the 21st century it will all have worn off.) Glass or stones are added for eyes, and some statues even get bronze accessories. The end results look so real, they can be a little creepy. You might think they looked more attractive before all that decoration.

Seeing a flowing figure appear from a block of stone is an almost supernatural experience (if you can wait around for two months).

What a relief

There's more to Greek sculpture than just statues, though. Sculptors also decorate slabs of stone by carving reliefs (scenes which stand out against a flat background).

You'll find them on temples mostly – check out the Parthenon for some fantastic examples. Or, for a more unusual art tour, visit the local graveyard, where you'll see some spectacular gravestones.

Paint me a picture

If you want to get a portrait done, there are lots of painters who'll be happy to oblige. They work on wooden panels, using paint that's mixed with eggs.

Mass production

It probably won't surprise you to hear that the best sculptors come from... you've guessed it: Athens. But as their fame spreads, the sculptors can't work fast enough to keep up with demand.

Sculptors make finishing touches to a relief for the local temple.

Now factories are springing up at quarries. Sculptures are produced on-site as quickly as possible, and then shipped off to art-lovers all over the Mediterranean.

These merchants may have bitten off more than they can chew.

A–grade architects

The Greeks are very proud of their temples. These buildings will make an impression on everyone, from the Romans (who'll copy everything they can get their hands on), to Renaissance Italians (who'll do exactly the same thing), to modern architects.

Greek architects calculate the height, width and proportions of buildings in advance. This gives them an air of balanced elegance. (Meaning, "they look good".)

Top tips for tourists

No. 13: Casing the joint

Avoid hanging around the back of a temple – it's where the treasury is located.

The guards won't be sympathetic if you say you're just an architecture fan, and Athenian jails are not fun places to visit.

Greek architects get to work, measuring a column block to make sure it's right.

66 Tough, useful, beautiful 99

The architecture-lover Vitruvius (a Roman) offers advice on what makes a good building.

Building blocks

Ask a Greek architect what he likes best in all the world, and he'll probably say columns. All public buildings have plenty of them, topped with horizontal beams (lintels), with the roof on top.

All in order

Thankfully, there is a little bit of variety. Most public buildings are designed in one of two different styles, known as "orders" - Doric and Ionic.

No-nonsense traditionalists prefer the Doric style. It's simple and straightforward, with broad, plain columns. The trendier Ionic style is fancy and decorative, with slender columns and finely carved capitals (the bits at the top of each column).

See how many examples of each order you can spot. You get extra points for Corinthian or Aeolic columns (both forms of the Ionic), because they're pretty rare.

Daring architects use *caryatids* – statues of women – instead of columns.

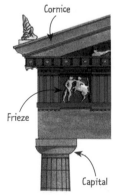

This temple is built in Doric style. The column is seriously sturdy, with no silly scrolls or carvings.

A new temple built in Ionic style. Note the curly capital that tops the column.

Capital capitals

A Corinthian capital for nature fans. It looks like a plant growing in a basket.

An Aeolic capital. Even stranger. The curly bits are supposed to be a ram's horns.

Let's stick together

Builders have to make do without cement – it's not been invented yet.

Instead, stone blocks are stuck together with pieces of metal called cramps. Column blocks have metal rods running through them, called dowels.

Touring a building site

Temples and other public buildings are being put up all the time, and a visit to a construction site can be a real eye-opener. The Acropolis in Athens is a great spot for this, since Pericles is having all of the temples there rebuilt.

The only things missing from the ancient skyline are cranes, but builders manage fine without them. It's well worth stopping for a while to watch them work. You'll gasp in amazement as massive stone blocks are lifted into place with ropes and pulleys. Just make sure you stand well back - accidents can be extremely unpleasant.

A temple building site

Some workers stand on wooden scaffolding, making sure the blocks go in the right place.

The stones are brought to the building site on wagons, and shaped on the ground with mallets and chisels.

Part three
Shop 'til you drop

There's no end of souvenirs to choose from in Ancient Greece. But it can be tricky picking just the right one, so read this section carefully if you're planning to splash out.

If you're a hardcore shopaholic, don't miss the Agora in the middle of Athens. Bargain hunters will be better off in Piraeus, the city's port, where you can pick up cut-price merchandise that "fell off the back of a ship".

Shoppers in Athens admire some high quality craftsmanship.

Market day

Ask anyone the way to the local *agora*, and you're bound to be pointed in the right direction. No wonder: it's the heart of every Greek city, where everyone who is anyone comes to pick up their olive oil, catch up on the juiciest gossip, and hear news of all the latest wars.

For a time tourist, it's the perfect place to stock up on supplies, get your bearings, and buy some gifts.

Fast food

Hungry? Don't worry – you can buy delicious snacks and hot food to go in the *agora*. Just don't expect burgers and hot dogs.

Be aware that eating in public is frowned upon (unless you happen to be a slave). If you're desperate for a quick bite and can't wait until lunchtime, sneak behind a column where no one can see you tucking in.

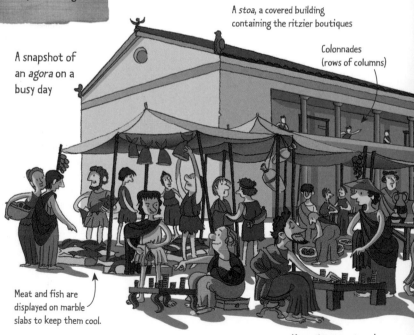

A snapshot of an *agora* on a busy day

A *stoa*, a covered building containing the ritzier boutiques

Colonnades (rows of columns)

Meat and fish are displayed on marble slabs to keep them cool.

Moneychangers at work

Shoppers' heaven

The market is mostly for food, but if you're keen to splash some cash, head for the covered buildings, which are called *stoae*. Behind colonnades (rows of columns to you and me) there are fancy stores offering everything from sparkling jewels to the latest in oil lamps. Storekeepers have all their wares behind the counter, so I'm afraid you can't really browse - you can only squint over their shoulders.

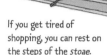

If you get tired of shopping, you can rest on the steps of the *stoae*.

Under the colonnades you can escape from the midday sun, meet friends and chat. Keep your ears open and you might overhear merchants making shady business deals, or sorting out the big political issues of the day.

Farmers setting out their stalls to sell their organic, fresh produce

This chicken is very fresh indeed.

Top tips for tourists

No. 14: In the money

Each time you arrive in a new city-state, you'll need to visit a moneychanger before you can shop. Ask for the *trapezitai* ("table men"), or look for the flashily dressed men sitting behind tables piled with coins.

These men change coins from every city-state, taking a small cut for themselves. Check your coins closely — worn ones will be rejected.

Athenian coins show an owl and an olive branch. Don't accept coins with any other kind of animal on them – they're probably fakes.

Top tips for tourists ♂

No. 15: Retail therapy – for men

A warning for female time tourists: in an *agora*, you won't be allowed to buy things costing more than a certain amount (the Greeks think that shopping is men's work). So take a male friend with you if you want to buy things.

It sounds pretty unfair, but look at it this way – at least you won't have to shop for boring things.

The produce police

Unfortunately, some stall holders aren't above trying to cheat a tourist every now and again. But help is on hand. If you think you're being fleeced, look out for one of the *agronomoi*. It's their job to look out for dodgy traders and make sure everyone's playing fair.

In Athens there are also ten *metronomoi* chosen each year to check the traders' weights and measures. That way they can make sure people are getting what they pay for.

These aren't just pots – they're measures, used by *metronomoi* to catch out crooked merchants.

People for sale

You can buy anything in an *agora* - and that includes people. You might be shocked, but the locals think that having slaves is perfectly natural - particularly if the slaves are defeated enemies. After all, they lost, so they deserve it.

A slave auction gets underway on a podium.

This is the slave seller, known as an *andrapodista*.

A rich citizen has sent his head slave to buy him more slaves.

Slaves for all occasions

The most expensive slaves are the ones with the most useful skills. Anyone who can play an instrument, cook well, or read and write is especially in demand. Once bought, they're looked after well - if they die on the job it's a real hassle, not to mention a big waste of money.

Others aren't so "lucky". Most of them end up working long hours on farms, in factories, or - worst of all - in a mine. And, if they've got a cruel master, they might easily starve - or be beaten to death.

Most Athenians own at least one slave. Slaves are often treated as part of the family – so long as they don't run away, that is.

A successful bidder heads home, happy with his new slave boy.

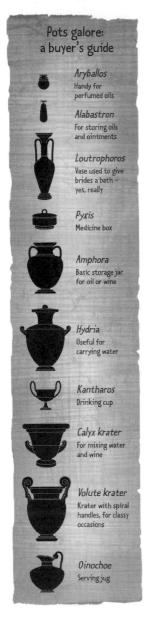

Pots galore: a buyer's guide

Aryballos
Handy for perfumed oils

Alabastron
For storing oils and ointments

Loutrophoros
Vase used to give brides a bath – yes, really

Pyxis
Medicine box

Amphora
Basic storage jar for oil or wine

Hydria
Useful for carrying water

Kantharos
Drinking cup

Calyx krater
For mixing water and wine

Volute krater
Krater with spiral handles, for classy occasions

Oinochoe
Serving jug

Pottering around

After your trip to the *agora*, it's worth taking a stroll past the shops of local craftsmen. Most of them live near the market, where they can attract lots of potential customers.

Craftsmen like to stick together, so there's an area for shoemakers, one for potters and so on - handy for comparing prices and styles. You can get things custom made too, so if you've always dreamed of having your portrait on a pot, you're in luck.

A buyer weighing up the pros and cons of a fine *amphora*.

Above all, don't miss the potters' workshops. Their wares are admired everywhere - or almost everywhere. The Persians have been rather less keen since Greek potters started painting rude pictures of them on their pots.

A potted history

Back in the Dark Ages, potters decorated their wares with simple patterns, adding in the odd human or animal if they were feeling really adventurous.

But things have come a long way since then. These days, potters have gone potty for detailed scenes from myth, history and daily life.

A good pot is painted in such detail, it's like a ready-made snapshot you can take home to show your friends. Much better than taking a camera, which will only attract unwelcome interest.

Early Dark Age designs were mostly just simple patterns – not much to look at.

Later designs included animals and humans – but still with lots of patterns.

Red is the new black

Many of the pots you'll see have black figures on a red background. It makes sense to do it this way, because the clay is red. But, lately, cutting-edge potters have been throwing caution to the winds and producing "red-figure ware" with - wait for it - red figures on a black background.

The pots are painted black, with spaces left for the figures. These bits turn red when the pot is baked in a kiln - a sort of giant oven.

The latest craze: "red-figure ware" with pictures of people. What will they think of next?

65

Impulse purchases are never a good idea.

Souvenir guide

My advice is to take your time when buying souvenirs. There are lots to choose from, and it's easy to get carried away and pick a gift that doesn't seem so wonderful once you get it back home.

Take a *krater*, for example. Such a familiar sight at Greek meals, and nice to look at... But put it in your parents' kitchen, and it'll probably just get in the way.

And that's not all. Even the trendiest Greek tunic will look dated by the time you get it back to the 21st century.

So read on for my tips on how to choose the perfect gift.

The perfect gift

First things first: go for light, easily portable items. (This may sound pretty obvious, but look at all the tourists struggling home through customs.)

How about a nice statuette or small piece of pottery? Hunt around a bit and you'll find something really special. Just be sure you don't end up paying a really special price for it.

66

Female friends and family might be pleased to receive rings or brooches (think "retro" - very retro), while music lovers are sure to appreciate a set of panpipes. It's not too hard to learn simple tunes on them, and they're a lot cheaper and easier to carry around than a lyre.

If you're stuck, there's always olive oil. Just make sure you pack it carefully, or you'll be stuck with soggy, greasy clothes, and no gift.

These quirky scent bottles are the pefect gift for anyone who likes perfume... and feet.

It's just what I wanted! A terracotta woman sitting in a bathtub

Looking for a personalized gift? Then commission a painting. If sculpture's more your thing, mini versions of temple carvings are available. They're supposed to be offerings for the gods, but they'd also make a nice offering for your grandma.

Top tips for tourists

No. 16: Sparing Granny's blushes

The Greeks have a very relaxed attitude to the human body – understandable in a place so hot you wear as little as possible. But it also means they're quite happy to plaster all sorts of dubious images over their pottery.

Many vases have very explicit scenes (red-figure ware in particular), so always check you've not got more than you bargained for. Unless you have broad-minded relatives, it might be safer to bring them back some olives.

A risqué wine cooler

Piraeus

66 *From all the lands, everything enters.* 99

Thucydides (politician and historian) sums up Piraeus in a nutshell.

Just 9 km (5½ miles) southwest of Athens lies the city's port, Piraeus. Lots of goods and souvenirs pass through here, before being carted off to Athens.

The place buzzes with activity. You can mingle with merchants, chat with sailors, or just bask in the sun, watching ship builders at work.

A busy day at the docks of Piraeus

These sailors are unloading sacks of wheat.

A wealthy customer admiring some imports

Fresh produce on sale

A thief, hard at work

Walk along the docks, and you'll bump into people from every nation. There are foreign sailors bringing all kinds of goods into Greece, and fellow tourists from Phoenicia, Egypt and Babylon.

Don't be surprised if you hear the locals calling them "barbarians" - it doesn't mean they think the visitors are savages. As tactless as it sounds, "barbarian" is the name that Greeks give to all foreigners. To them, all foreign languages just sound like "baa-baa, baa-baa..."

Top tips for tourists

No. 17: Last minute bargains

If you're still stuck for souvenirs, Piraeus is a top spot to find last-minute mementos. For bargain prices (with no refunds), warehouses sell items that didn't survive the journey too well.

Loading a cargo of oil onto a cart, for transporting to the warehouse

Catch of the day: fish is plentiful and very fresh.

Cooking lunch for the sailors, dockhands and tourists

Another thief at work

Clever Themistocles

It was a shrewd politician named Themistocles who persuaded the Athenians to make the most of Piraeus. He ordered a wall to be built round the port in 493BC, turned it into a naval headquarters, and had the whole place redesigned to make the best use of its three bays. Now that the Athenian navy rules the waves, everyone agrees that it was a pretty smart idea.

Piraeus in peril

Not to be outdone, all-round hero Pericles is currently having massive walls built all along the road from Athens to Piraeus. This should stop any attackers cutting off the city from the port. After a good, hard think, Pericles has decided to call these long walls "The Long Walls".

Thanks to Pericles, the Long Walls are turning the city of Athens into a fortress.

Part four
Trips out of Athens

Alright, I'll admit it - there are some things that even the great city of Athens can't offer. Who'd want to miss out on a visit to Olympia, to see the famous Games? Or if you like hard work (or watching it, at least), explore the silver mines at Laurion, a major source of the Athenian's wealth. You could even visit an Oracle to hear what the future holds in store for you.

But, be warned! Never, under any circumstances, go anywhere near Sparta. You can find out why on pages 84-86...

This charioteer is honing his skills for the Olympics.

Fun and games?

The Olympic Games are great fun to watch, but you should know that they can be violent.

Almost all the events are dangerous in one way or another, and it's not unknown for athletes to be killed. Horse racing is one of the worst – jockeys often fall off and get trampled to death.

The Olympics ♂

If you like sport, don't miss the original Olympic Games. As long as you're male, that is. I'm afraid female time tourists won't be welcome.

The Games began way back in 776BC. Other games have started since, but the Olympics are still the biggest and the best. They're dedicated to Zeus, and held at Olympia every four years, lasting five days. Messengers travel to every Greek state to announce the date. The whole thing is taken so seriously that wars are called off to allow tourists to travel to Olympia safely.

Once you arrive, there's lots to see and do besides the Games themselves: souvenir stalls along the roads, shrines to visit, sightseeing tours, and poetry recitals. You can even use the pool - as long as there are no athletes in it.

The Olympic village

Training area for jumping and wrestling

The Gymnasium: a training ground for running and throwing events

Temple of Hera

Treasuries holding money and valuable objects

Temple of Zeus

The stadium

Hippodrome for chariot and horse races

Guide to the best events

Running: the oldest event. The stadium track is 192m (640ft) long, made of clay covered with sand. There are three races: 1 length, 2 lengths and 20 or 24 lengths.

Wrestling: there are three types: "upright", where an opponent must be thrown to the ground three times; "ground", which goes on until one someone gives in; and "*pankration*", which is very nasty – anything goes except biting and eye-gouging.

Boxing: you'll need almost as much stamina as the fighters, as boxing matches last for hours. They're only decided when someone gives up or loses consciousness – so most blows are aimed at the head, and contestants can be as violent as they like.

Chariot & horse racing: chariot drivers race 12 laps around two posts in the ground, while jockeys ride bareback over 1.2km (¾ mile).

Pentathlon: made up of five events – running, wrestling, jumping, discus and javelin throwing. This one gets extremely competitive, because the winner is thought to be the best all-round athlete.

WARNING! In real life, athletes don't bother with clothes. They wear nothing but a layer of oil, to protect against the sun.

73

Ready, steady, go!

The stadium is full to bursting. A trumpet sounds, the judges take their seats... and the Games begin.

The first event kicks off with another lot of trumpet blasts (don't stand too near the musicians), and a herald announcing the race. Then he calls out the names of the competitors (who are all men). This is important, because only citizens who've never committed a crime can take part. At the end of each event, he'll also announce the name of the winner, his father's name and which city he comes from.

The first day begins with track events, while the other events are spread out over the next four days. Don't miss the chariot races in the hippodrome. They're very popular, so you'll need to get there early for a good position.

If you're sick of the crowds, you can
watch the Games in peace from the
grassy slopes around the stadium.

Prize performances

Prizes are awarded on the last day: ribbons, olive wreaths and palm branches. It might sound stingy, but the glory of victory is supposed to be enough. Actually, a winning athlete gets far bigger rewards after the Games. His home city gains prestige from the victory, and city officials show their gratitude with large "gifts" on the quiet.

City officials show their appreciation to a winning athlete.

Wreathed in glory

Every athlete worth his salt dreams of winning one of the coveted olive leaf wreaths. They might not keep the rain off, but they're made with the leaves of a sacred tree that grows in the Olympic grounds.

The wreath itself soon withers away, but the glory of winning lasts for a lifetime. Some athletes even get statues of themselves in their local *agora*.

Games for girls

Married women are banned from watching the Olympics (so they don't see all those naked athletes), and single women aren't welcome either. Female time tourists can go to the *Heraia* festival instead, which is women-only. It has running races, but no chariot racing or wrestling.

This statue shows a woman in training for the *Heraia*. In the real thing, the women compete naked, just as the men do.

Seeing the future

Stuck on what to do next? In that case, now is a good time to visit an oracle. It's where the Greeks go if they need a spot of advice from the gods.

As well as the place, "oracle" is also the name for the priestess who delivers advice on the god's behalf. Naturally, gods are very busy - they can't do everything themselves.

A messenger delivers an oracle's advice to a politician.

Apollo's oracle

I can recommend the oracle at Delphi, built around a sacred spring on the slopes of Mount Parnassus. It's the god Apollo who offers his advice there, via a priestess called a Pythia. In fact, this oracle has now become so popular that two extra Pythias have recently been taken on. (There's still only one Apollo, of course.)

Once you've climbed the mountain, you can ask anything. The Pythias have heard it all - from "where is my nice *amphora*?" to "should I declare war on Sparta?"

But first, you'll have to make a sacrifice, to see if Apollo takes a shine to you. If you pass this test, you'll join a long line of answer-seekers.

> 66 *Unhappy people, why stay you here? Leave your homes... and flee to the ends of the Earth.* 99
>
> Herodotus, a historian, reporting the Pythia's encouraging words to the Athenians just before a Persian attack

Go-betweens

Before you ask your question, take a quick dip in the Castalian Spring - Apollo is a stickler for cleanliness. Then you pass your question on to a priest, and he brings the answer back from the Pythia.

You can't speak directly with the Pythia - she's too busy speaking to Apollo. But this picture should give you an idea what goes on.

Even the priests of Delphi can't watch the Pythia at work. She's hidden behind a curtain.

The Pythia sits on a tripod and inhales the smoke of burning laurel leaves. Then she goes into a trance and gives Apollo's answer.

Which diviner?

A seer reads the future from a set of tokens with symbolic signs.

An augur reads signs in nature – in the flight of birds, for example.

A haruspex has a really revolting job: "reading" the innards of a sacrificed animal.

The omen

If Delphi is too far out of your way, ask where the local diviner (reader of signs) lives. They come in three varieties, which you can see on the left. You'll have to pay for their services, and unlike Apollo, the omens can only say "yes" or "no".

Soothsayers

For a more detailed answer, try the nearest soothsayer. They can actually see into the future. Not convinced? Then have you heard the story of Cassandra? She foretold that the Greeks would destroy Troy, even though they had sailed away and given the Trojans a giant wooden horse. No one believed her - until Greeks spilled out of the horse's belly...

Cassandra told them so, but did they listen?

78

Mystery cults

Stranger still are "mystery cults", whose members claim to know the meaning of life. You might be intrigued, but I should warn you that they're very secretive, and you can't just stroll into a meeting.

If you fancy a sneak peek, you can watch a procession: every September, members of the Eleusinian Cult walk from Athens to Eleusis.

Members of the Eleusinian Cult arrive in Eleusis at night, with torches to light the way.

Initiation

Whatever you do, don't be tempted to join a mystery cult. They're called that for a reason - it's a complete mystery what happens when you join.

Take the Eleusinian Cult, for instance. New members have to enter the mysterious Telesterion temple in Eleusis for their initiation. No one knows what's inside...

An excuse to be rude

One of the strangest traditions of the Eleusinian procession is to sing rude and insulting songs to fellow cult members. This is to show respect for Iambe, the goddess of rude poems.

A silver lining

> **" There is silver in the earth — a gift of the gods, no doubt. Indeed, in the many states near to Athens by land and by sea, not one of them has even the slightest trace of silver ore. "**
>
> Xenophon, proud Athenian and silver enthusiast

If you don't want to spend your holiday visiting oracles and soothsayers, you might like a trip to the silver mines at Laurion, south of Athens.

Much of the city's wealth is thanks to this mine, and its rich seam of silver-lead. Laurion is the largest silver supplier in the ancient world, so the Athenians are lucky it's on their turf (well, under it, at least).

A peek inside the mine
(Visitors are banned from going down.)

Miners climb down a very narrow shaft to get in.

They often have to crawl into tiny spaces and work on their backs.

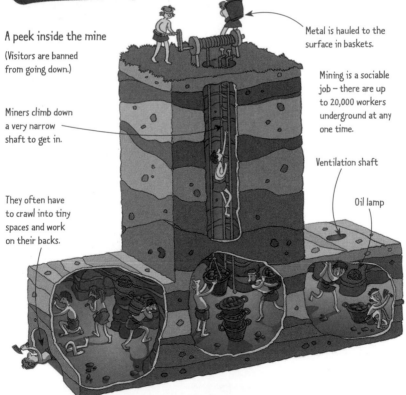

Metal is hauled to the surface in baskets.

Mining is a sociable job — there are up to 20,000 workers underground at any one time.

Ventilation shaft

Oil lamp

Staying grounded

You won't be allowed to go underground, but don't worry, you probably wouldn't want to anyway - especially if you're at all claustrophobic. And there's plenty to see on the surface.

The silver-lead ore leaves the mine with a lot of mine still on it. So, the next stage is getting rid of the debris. Slaves pound the ore with clubs, to break it up from the rock. This is a dusty business, so bring a light scarf to cover your face if you want to see the slaves in action.

Next, the crumbly mix is flooded with water and sifted, to rinse the rock dust from the ore. Finally, the ore goes into a furnace, where fierce temperatures extract the silver from the lead. After that, the metal is ready to be shaped.

Breaking up the rock and silver-lead ore

Worked to death

Working at Laurion is no picnic. Slaves work ten-hour shifts in terrible, cramped conditions, to get as much silver as fast as possible. It's so tough that most of them die after just three or four years on the job.

Top tips for tourists

No. 21: Tipping tips

Some slaves in Athens (usually craftsmen), are paid for their work. So if you're happy with the goods or service provided, it's perfectly fine to tip them – after all, the money will help buy their freedom.

But in Laurion the mine owners don't want the slaves even to have a chance of leaving. Slip a slave money and you'll get him into trouble with his overseer.

" He threw hard copper on the fire, and tin... Then he put his giant anvil on its block and took his big hammer... **"**

Top poet Homer describing Hephaestos, god of smiths, at work

Bronzed off

Silver is pricey stuff, so most everyday metal objects are made with bronze - a mixture of tin and copper. If you don't have time for Laurion, you could go and watch a metalsmith in action instead. Here's a rundown of their top techniques:

Hammering method

Hammering method: sheets of bronze are bashed into shape around a wooden core, then riveted together. It's only the older smiths who bother with this. It's time-consuming and the results don't look great.

Casting method

Casting method: melted bronze is poured into a cast - a hollow space that's the shape of the object being made. Then it's left to harden. If you're watching, don't ask distracting questions while the pouring takes place. Molten bronze hurts a LOT if it gets poured on your foot.

Lost wax method: model of a boy riding a dolphin

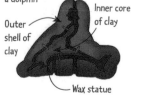

Outer shell of clay

Inner core of clay

Wax statue

Lost wax method: a wax statue is shaped around a clay core, then covered in more clay and heated until the wax melts and can be poured out. Then bronze is poured in instead. Once this has solidified, the outer clay is removed, to reveal a perfectly formed bronze statue.

Iron smiths sweating it out by a furnace

Layers of charcoal and iron ore are put in the brick furnace.

This man is pumping bellows, to make the fire burn even hotter.

This man has to concentrate – he's holding a very hot piece of metal.

The iron is hammered while it's red hot, to remove impurities.

Ironed out

The Greeks have been using iron for about 500 years. It's the metal of choice for weapons and tools, because it's so tough and can be made very sharp. Iron hasn't replaced bronze yet though, as it's much more expensive to produce. Smiths have to heat the iron ore at a very high temperature to extract the metal, before bashing out the impurities with a big hammer.

Precious metals

Smiths make things from gold and silver too, but not many people can actually afford them. Most of the silver from Laurion ends up in coins and in luxury goods, bought by very wealthy showoffs.

Spartan territory
Spartan occupied land
States allied to Sparta
Independent states

This map of the Peloponnesian League shows how the Spartans rule the roost.

A bronze statue of a Spartan warrior. You wouldn't want to meet him in a dark alley... or anywhere else.

Sparta: keep out!

Most of Ancient Greece is fairly safe for time tourists (as long as you stick to the towns, and aren't a Persian). But whatever you do, don't go to Sparta.

Spartans are obsessed with war. They spend their entire time training to be the toughest and nastiest fighters in Greece. And they REALLY don't like foreigners. Trust me, it's not a good place for a relaxing vacation.

Hard as nails

So who are these Spartans anyway? Well, the city of Sparta is the strongest military power in Greece - hardly surprising considering how much they love fighting. They're also in charge of a group of states known as the Peloponnesian League. That means they can "borrow" soldiers from these states whenever they like.

It's a Spartan man's duty to be ready for battle at a moment's notice, and they spend their lives training for war. Everyone eats horrible food and wears cheap clothes to keep them in a really nasty mood. That way, they never soften up.

Tough love

A Spartan's hard life starts at birth. In fact, if you're a weakling you don't even get a life. Babies that aren't strong enough are just left outside to die. The boys that survive are sent to live in barracks and train for war - at only the age of seven.

Women's rights

Spartan women get to play sports, at least (unlike in the rest of Greece). That's because they have to keep fit to have healthy babies - preferably boys, who can join the army. They have to bring up the children, and they only see their husbands on rare weekend leave from the barracks.

Spartan women are the toughest in Greece.

Spartan "schools"

In the barracks, Spartan boys are put into groups. Then they choose a leader to be in charge.

For the next 13 years, they have non-stop weapons training, fitness sessions and beatings to check their toughness.

They're encouraged to fight each other to protect their reputations – and their tunics (they only get one a year).

Top tips
for tourists

No. 22: If you ignore all of my advice...

...and do go to Sparta, be warned. On your return to Athens (if you return), you won't be greeted with open arms – more likely a spear point. The Athenians don't really trust the Spartans, and with good reason: a vicious war will break out between the two cities in 431BC.

Not one of us

Being a Spartan is like being in a very exclusive club - you have to be born in the city itself to be a citizen. These "proper" Spartans leave it to the people who live in the surrounding villages to deal with trade and outsiders. They don't want any distraction from their training.

This means that even if you did go to Sparta (please don't), you might not actually meet a Spartan. In fact, the Spartans are so cut off from the rest of the world that they don't even have money - they just swap things instead.

A hard life for helots

A Spartan soldier, on a rare visit home, checks up on a helot slave on his farm.

If you need one last example of how savage the Spartans are, look at the helots. They were living on Spartan land long before the Spartans got there, but the newcomers treat them like slaves. Each Spartan soldier has a plot of land, and helots to work it, so he can concentrate on fighting. It's a convenient arrangement - as long as you're not one of the helots.

Part five
Greece: the lowdown

Remember the first rule of time tourism?
That's it – Always Blend In. Well, you'll
find this a lot easier if you know your
hoplites from your *himations*.

Confused? You'd better read on if you
don't want to risk the wrath of Zeus
(especially if you're not sure who Zeus
is). The local knowledge in this section
will make your trip more interesting,
soften the culture shock, and might even
save you from a major faux-pas...

This is Zeus,
to remind you.

Democratic divisions

Democracy is a complex business. Athenian land is split into many small areas called *demes*...

↓

...which are organized into 30 large groups called *trittyes*. That's:

10 groups on the coast,

10 in the city (Athens),

and 10 in the country.

↓

This is where it gets confusing: the *trittyes* are split into 10 *phylai*. Each has 3 *trittyes*: 1 each from the country, the city and the coast:

Who's in charge?

Greece is often called the birthplace of democracy. The word actually comes from the Greek words for "people" (*demos*) and "rule" (*kratos*). It sounds great - but as far as the Athenians are concerned, the only people that count are free men with Athenian parents. Women, slaves and foreigners can't even vote.

If you think that's unfair though, it could be worse. Athens used to be ruled by a group of nobles, and before that, by a king who could do whatever he wanted. For some Greek cities this hasn't changed. In fact, the Spartans have two kings, so they can keep an eye on each other. Most kings are rather nervous of the Athenians - democracy could put them out of a job.

The nitty gritty

The democratic system was invented by Cleisthenes, leader of Athens, in 506BC. Cunning Cleisthenes split all the people in the city and its surrounding lands (known as Attica) into small communities called *demes*, to make it easier to govern them. You can see how this works on the left.

88

Town council

It might be "rule by the people", but that doesn't mean any citizen can make up laws or declare war if they've had a bad day.

The Council, made up of 500 men, puts forward new laws. Then their proposals are debated in the Assembly, where every citizen is allowed to speak and vote. By now, you'll know how much the Greeks love talking, so you'll see how this takes a very long time.

The members of the Council meet close to the Agora in Athens, inside this round building. It's called the Tholos.

All the same, if you want to see democracy in action, the Assembly meets on the Pnyx Hill about every ten days. It'll be crowded - 6,000 citizens are needed for a meeting to take place at all. If too few turn up, police just go and round up more voters. Don't get carried away and try to vote yourself. You'll be thrown out.

The *Polemarch Archon* takes care of offerings for men killed in war, and foreign residents' rights.

The *Basileus Archon* is the go-to man for law courts, sacrifices and renting out temple land.

The *Eponymous Archon* chooses *choregoi* (rich sponsors) for drama festivals, and is in charge of inheritance and family law.

Friends in high places

If you get into trouble while staying in Athens, there are a few people you could go to who might be able to help you out.

For starters, there are nine *archons*. They mostly just take part in ceremonies, but three of them have special jobs. (You can see what each man is in charge of on the left.)

Your best bet is the *Polemarch Archon*. Since he's responsible for foreign people living in the city, he should at least be sympathetic to a tourist.

Soldier politicians

Look out for the *strategoi*. There are ten of them, and they're the top dogs in Athens.

Why are they so powerful? Because it's their job to implement the policies approved by the Assembly. That, and the fact that they're in command of the entire Athenian army and navy. If you meet one, be careful not to get on the wrong side of him.

Of course, even the *strategoi* have to let the Assembly know what they're up to (especially if they're spending large amounts of money - or planning a big war).

Banished!

The Athenians don't put up with bad politicians for long. Once a year, they get together in the Assembly to banish any they don't like.

These *ostraka* show that Aristides and Kimon are in danger of being ostracised.

It's worth going along to watch, if you're in Athens at the right time. Everyone writes the name of someone they want kicked out of the city on a piece of pot called an *ostrakon*. If someone has more than 600 votes against him, he is "ostracised" - which means he must leave Athens for 10 years.

Ask a citizen about ostracism and he'll soon tell you the tale of Aristides. There was a citizen who wanted to vote for Aristides to be ostracised, but he couldn't write. So, he asked a stranger to write the name for him. Unfortunately, the stranger was Aristides himself - but he wrote his name anyway.

Aristides writes his own name on an *ostrakon*, on behalf of a citizen who can't write.

Foreign policy

The Athenians are a proud lot, but you'll know by now that they're worried about the ever-present threat of the Persians (and Spartans). You might hear talk of the Delian League - it's an alliance of Greek states, including Athens, to protect each other.

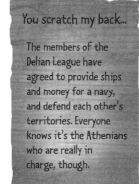

You scratch my back...

The members of the Delian League have agreed to provide ships and money for a navy, and defend each other's territories. Everyone knows it's the Athenians who are really in charge, though.

Shielded from harm

If you're in a really tight spot, you could invest in a shield. Most cover the body from the neck to the thigh. A soldier usually has a symbol of his family or city on it.

Military matters

However careful you are, there's a danger that you'll get stuck in a city that's at war. If this happens, it might comfort you to know that Greek soldiers are feared throughout the ancient world. (Of course, this might not be so comforting if they're fighting another lot of Greeks.)

You'll know there's a war if you see hoplites around town. They're a type of elite foot soldier, highly trained and extremely well equipped.

Spot the hoplite

The modern hoplite is a fully fledged fighting machine, kitted out in bronze and leather protection, complete with bronze leg guards and a gigantic shield made out of... bronze and leather.

A hoplite's main weapon is a long spear that's good for thrusting, jabbing and stabbing. If it breaks, he's got a short iron sword. You might be surprised to hear that the hoplite buys this expensive equipment himself. But it's worth it - he'd soon be dead without it.

A hoplite gets ready for battle

3m (10ft) spear of bronze

Body protector, called a cuirass

Leg guards, known as greaves

Iron sword with wooden handle

Ready for battle

A Greek army on the way to battle is an impressive sight. In particular, you'll be struck by the hoplites' bronze helmets, with their elegant horsehair plumes.

Most hoplites will be wearing Thracian helmets, but you might spot some older designs (like the Corinthian and Chalcidian on the right). They're worn by die-hard traditionalists, and by wimps who want to have more of their face covered.

Thracian helmet

Corinthian helmet

Chalcidian helmet

Auxiliaries

If someone suggests that you help out and join the *psiloi*, whatever you do, say "no". These are the men who can't afford a hoplite's gear, and have to fight with stones, clubs and whatever they can get.

Call up

Fortunately for you, it's usually just Greek men that have to fight. In Athens, there's the "List": all citizens aged between 20 and 50 are on it, and have to fight if there's a war – which is often. In a real emergency, men aged up to 60 are called up, too.

66 *Fight shield to shield and never give in to panic or miserable flight, but steel the heart in your chest with magnificence and courage.* 99

The Spartan poet Tyrtaeus giving battle advice (from well behind the front line)

Phantastic phalanx

Hopefully, you won't ever have to see the secret of the hoplites' amazing success in battle. But in case you're curious, it's a battle formation called the phalanx. The hoplites fight in a huge block, eight rows deep, shields locked together, so that the enemy is faced with a virtually unstoppable wall of bronze.

That's enough to make many enemies turn and run - unless the enemy is another lot of Greeks. In that case, the opposing phalanxes just charge together and shove each other as hard as they can. Eventually, one side will give way and flee.

In a phalanx, every hoplite is protected by the shield of the next man. Except for the man on the end...

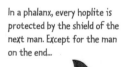

Runners

Soldiers from Thrace, known as peltasts, have worked out a way of beating the phalanx. They throw javelins at it until it breaks up, then pick off the hoplites one by one. So young hoplites known as *ekdromoi* sometimes run ahead to chase off the peltasts.

Besieged

If you're unlucky, you might get caught in a city that's under siege. This means it's surrounded by enemy troops, who let no one in or out. The idea is to starve the citizens into surrender. It often backfires though, with the besieging army starving too - or just dying of boredom.

If you're really unlucky though, the enemy might have brought siege weapons. You can see two of them below. You might recognize them as medieval weapons, but believe me, the Greeks were there first.

Tower power

If the attackers can get inside a city, it's all over. The easiest way is to get a citizen to betray the city and let them in.

A less subtle approach is to use a siege tower, which protects soldiers while they scale walls, with catapults firing arrows and hurling rocks from the ground.

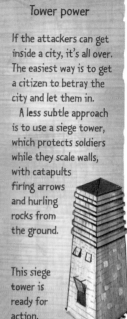

This siege tower is ready for action.

A battering ram is a good way of breaking down city gates.

Wooden covering

Wooden beam

It's got a wooden covering in case defenders throw things at the soldiers below.

This flamethrower is like a nastier version of the ram. It's used to spray fire onto buildings from a swinging cauldron.

Air is pumped down a hollow tree trunk to feed the fire.

Hollow tree trunk

Bellows

Sea dogs

Not only do the Greeks have top notch armies, they're no slouches when it comes to sea battles, either. If you're in a coastal town, see if you can spot a trireme or two in the harbour. It's the mainstay of a Greek fleet, powered by sails and, unlike merchant vessels, a crew of oarsmen. That way commanders don't have to put off a battle just because there's no wind.

With three rows of oars, the trireme is literally three times better than earlier warships - which had just one row each.

Some triremes have 85 oarsmen on either side, so they can go very fast indeed.

The strongest rowers, known as the *thranites*, sit on the highest level. Below them are the *zygites*, and the *thalamites*.

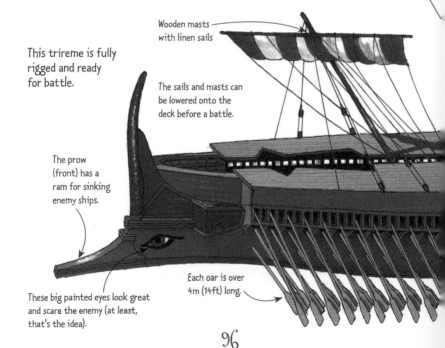

This trireme is fully rigged and ready for battle.

Wooden masts with linen sails

The sails and masts can be lowered onto the deck before a battle.

The prow (front) has a ram for sinking enemy ships.

These big painted eyes look great and scare the enemy (at least, that's the idea).

Each oar is over 4m (14ft) long.

96

Manpower

Each trireme can carry a crew of up to 200 men, mostly recruited from the poorer classes. All but 30 are rowers. The rest are officers, deckhands, archers and soldiers.

Being on a trireme isn't much fun. Conditions are very cramped, and there are no luxury cabins or deck chairs to relax in. But the crews don't seem to mind.

They're happy knowing that triremes are the most powerful warships in the Mediterranean.

Ship's captain

Every year in Athens a rich citizen is chosen to adopt a trireme (meaning, pay for it). He's known as the ship's *trierarch*.

Technically the *trierarch* is the captain of the ship, but if he's sensible he'll get someone else – who actually knows what he's doing – to go to sea in his place.

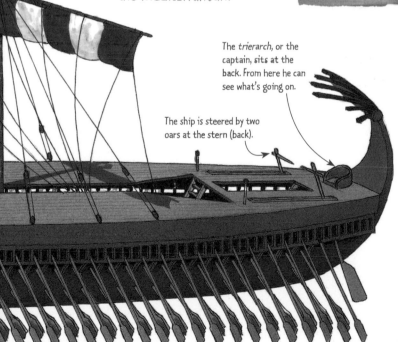

The *trierarch*, or the captain, sits at the back. From here he can see what's going on.

The ship is steered by two oars at the stern (back).

How to sink a ship

Sweep round the enemy line and launch a sneak attack from behind.

Swerve in suddenly, sweeping past the enemy ship and breaking all its oars.

Swing to the side at the last moment, ramming straight into the side of the enemy ship.

For the very daring: dart through a gap in the line of ships, and curve round behind.

Bloody seas

Don't be tempted to hitch a lift on a trireme. You don't want to end up in a sea battle – they can be even more violent than ones on the land.

In the past, a captain would order his oarsmen to row as fast as possible, and ram the enemy ship. Then his archers would rain arrows on the enemy crew, before he sent in his soldiers to finish off the survivors in hand-to-hand combat. Simple and effective – and best of all, no one could run away.

Tricky triremes

Thanks to triremes, things have got more complicated. These ships are nippy, and easy to steer. If the oarsmen are rowing in time, the vessel can start, stop and turn rapidly, and go at 15km (9 miles) an hour.

This means that a trireme captain can attack enemy ships from all kinds of sneaky, unexpected angles – including the sides and stern (that's the back).

Some things don't change, though. Once the enemy has been rammed, the captain gets his soldiers to kill everyone onboard.

The Battle of Salamis

If you find yourself chatting to a nautical Greek, you'll impress him if you mention the Battle of Salamis - the Greeks' most brilliant naval victory against the Persians.

Before the battle, the oracle at Delphi said the Greeks would win if they trusted in their "wooden walls" - the triremes. The oracle got it right. The Greeks trapped a much larger Persian fleet between two straits of land, and sank hundreds of ships.

66 I'm from where the good triremes come from. 99

An Athenian boasts about his city's navy in a play by Aristophanes (an Athenian).

If the danger of battle doesn't put you off, look at this trireme in a storm...

Triremes are less stable when the sails are up. In bad weather, they're very vulnerable.

This *trierarch* is wishing he'd stayed at home.

Captain

Everyone is hoping to bring the ship in safely – there are no cooking or sleeping facilities, so the ship must land by nightfall.

These oarsmen are wearing clothes, but a lot of rowers are naked – especially in hot weather.

Gods & goddesses

You won't get anywhere in Ancient Greece unless you know about the Immortals, the gods and goddesses who watch over everyone. They're as familiar to the Greeks as their own families - and even more difficult to deal with. There are lots of stories to explain how to please them, so they don't turn you into a toad - or worse.

In the beginning...

...Gaea (Mother Earth) arose out of chaos. She had a son, Uranos (Sky), and married him (the gods are a strange bunch). They had lots of children, including 14 called Titans. One of these, Cronos, kicked out his dad and married his sister Rhea.

They had several children, and the youngest son, Zeus, followed family tradition by getting rid of dad and marrying his sister Hera. Then he led his brothers and sisters in a war against their aunts and uncles, the Titans, and beat them. Nowadays he and his siblings rule from Mount Olympus. This earned them the nickname, the Olympians.

Half man, half god

You might meet Greeks who claim to have a god for a father and a human for a mother (or vice versa). These lucky individuals are called demi-gods (if you believe them).

The most famous was Heracles. You might have heard of him by his Roman name – Hercules. The son of Zeus and a mortal woman named Alcmene, Heracles had superhuman strength. When he died, Zeus made him a proper god.

Zeus gets ready to hurl one of his dreaded thunderbolts.

100

Holy who's who

Zeus: king of the gods, married to Hera. That doesn't stop him from indulging in various flings with mortal women, though. His symbols are a thunderbolt, an eagle and an oak tree.

Hera: wife (and sister) of Zeus and protector of women and marriage. She's beautiful but proud and jealous. Her symbols are a cuckoo, a pomegranate and a peacock.

Poseidon: brother of Zeus and ruler of the sea. He lives underwater and is said to cause earthquakes, hence his nickname, "Earth-shaker". His symbols are a trident (three-pronged fork), dolphins and horses.

Hestia: goddess of the hearth. There's a shrine to her in every Greek home. She's gentle and pure, and keeps out of her relatives' constant quarrels.

Ares: son of Zeus and Hera and god of war. He's young, strong and handsome but with a violent temper - not helped by the fact that he's constantly looking for a fight. His symbols are a burning torch, a spear, dogs and vultures.

Top tips
for tourists

No. 23: Master of disguise

Zeus is thought to go to extreme lengths when chasing mortal women. In the past, he's said to have disguised himself as a bull, a swan, and even a shower of gold.
  So if you're a female time tourist, be sure not to speak to strange animals – you never know, it could be Zeus on the prowl.

Hestia

Hephaestos

Hephaestos: son of Zeus and Hera, he's a first-class blacksmith with some amazing tricks up his sleeve - he once built a shield for his father which causes thunder and storms whenever it's shaken. His forge lies beneath the volcanic Mount Etna on Sicily. He's the patron of craftsmen and husband of Aphrodite, goddess of love, though he's not much of a looker himself.

Artemis: the moon goddess, she loves to go hunting with her silver arrows. But she's a great healer too, and protects young girls, pregnant women and wild animals - when she's not busy hunting them. Her symbols are cypress trees, deer and dogs.

Dionysus: god of wine and fertility, this is one god who doesn't take himself too seriously. He spends his time roaming the countryside, holding wild parties with his followers, and he's only allowed to sit on Mount Olympus when Hestia is away.

Aphrodite

Aphrodite: goddess of love and beauty, and a born troublemaker, she may be married to Hephaestos but she'd rather be with hunky Ares. Born in the sea, she rode to shore on a scallop shell. She's a real charmer, though some say that's thanks to her magic golden belt. Her symbols are roses and doves.

Hermes: when he was a young scamp, he stole some cattle from Apollo. So, to keep him out of mischief, Zeus made him the messenger of the gods. It's up to him to take care of you - he's the patron of tourists (and thieves). He has a pair of wings on his hat, and one on his shoes, just in case.

Athene: one day, Zeus had a terrible headache. No wonder - the next minute, the goddess Athene sprang from his head, fully armed. She's the goddess of wisdom and war, and the patron of Athens. Her symbols are an owl and an olive tree.

Apollo: the twin brother of Artemis, he's the god of sun, light and truth, not to mention music, poetry, science and healing. His shrine at Delphi is on the spot where he killed his mother's enemy, Python the serpent. His symbol is the laurel tree.

Pluto: Zeus's brother, he doesn't see much of the other gods - he's ruler of the Underworld, land of the dead. He guards his subjects closely, rarely letting any return to the land of the living. He owns all precious metals and gems on Earth.

Hermes

Apollo

Pluto

103

Funeral march

If you're out early, you may come across a funeral procession. Most set off before dawn for cemeteries outside the city.

Don't be alarmed by the emotions on display. The Greeks show their grief with wailing, ripping of clothes and tearing of hair.

Some families hire extra mourners and musicians, which makes even more of a racket.

Life after death

The Greeks believe that people's souls live on after death - but only if the funeral rites are performed properly.

So when someone dies, his or her relatives wash the body, douse it in fragrant oils and dress it in white. They lie it out on display for a day, so that friends can come and pay their respects. If you see people wearing black, and women with their hair cut short, that's where they're heading.

On the day of the funeral, a coin is put in the dead person's mouth, and the body is carried in a cart to its tomb.

R.I.P.

The body is then burned or buried with ancestors in the family plot, together with personal belongings such as clothes and jewels. There's even food and drink, for use in the afterlife.

Rich Greeks are buried in stone coffins, and some have tombs the size of small temples. You might spot family members bringing food to the tomb. They're probably not going for a picnic - they'll be leaving offerings for the dead person.

A graveyard is worth a visit to see stone markers (*stelae*) like this one, with reliefs of the dead person and their family.

Journey to Hades

Hermes

The Greeks think that the souls of the dead go to an underground world called Hades. This is one trip you should certainly try to avoid taking while you're in Ancient Greece. But just so you know, here's what the Greeks think happens to a soul, after the body has been buried:

1. Hermes, messenger of the gods, guides the soul to the River Styx, which divides the worlds of the living and the dead.

Charon, the ferryman

2. The soul pays Charon, the ferryman, to take him or her over the river to the entrance of Hades. (Souls without a coin are stuck on the bank forever.)

3. The soul skirts past Cerberus, a three-headed guard dog.

Cerberus

4. Next stop is a crossroads, where three judges pass a verdict on the person's life. The soul is sent to one of three places for eternity – turn the page to find out more.

The judges make their decision.

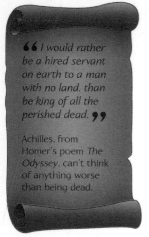

The Asphodel Meadows

Souls who haven't been especially good or bad in life are sent to the Asphodel Meadows. Most people end up here. It's a dull place, where souls just wander around with nothing to do (imagine being stuck at home... forever). They drink from the Pool of Lethe, which makes the drinker forget his or her past life.

Tartarus

Meanwhile, souls who have been extremely wicked or cruel go straight to Tartarus, where they face eternal torture. The Greeks love imagining all kinds of horrible punishments that take place there. You can see a few below.

Bored souls in the Asphodel Meadows

Unpleasant punishments in Tartarus

106

Peculiar punishments

Some of the punishments are a little strange, though. For instance, the daughters of Danaus, who murdered their husbands, have to spend their whole time filling up a big pot with water - but the pot has a hole in it. Meanwhile, a man named Ixion, who tried to run away with Zeus' wife Hera, is tied to a burning wheel of fire that never stops spinning.

The Elysian Fields

People who've led a really good life don't need to worry about all this. Their souls spend all eternity in the Elysian Fields, singing, dancing and generally enjoying being dead.

The Isle of the Blessed

The only people who have it better than that are the members of mystery cults, who can choose to be reborn. If they die and reach the Elysian Fields three times, they get to go to the Isle of the Blessed, a place of everlasting joy. The afterlife doesn't get better than that.

The living dead

It's probably best to steer clear of the underworld unless you're actually dead, but there are some stories about people going there and coming back alive.

Two of the most famous are the musician Orpheus, who tried to rescue his dead wife, and the hero Heracles, who went there to kidnap the guard dog Cerberus.

After three lives, a rest is in order.

107

Happy families?

Whether you're a female or a male time tourist, you'll probably have noticed that it's not much fun being a woman in Ancient Greece. They're banned from voting, can't go to parties, and spend most of the time doing what they're told.

Take weddings, for instance. A girl is married at 15, to a groom of her father's choice (often twice her age). She even comes with a free gift of cash from her dad, to say thanks for taking her off his hands.

Often, the couple meet for the first time at the wedding. So, if you meet a man or woman who's engaged, don't be surprised if they're more nervous than excited.

Dads don't always pick the best husbands for their daughters.

'Til divorce do us part

A divorced woman keeps the money and goods she brought from her dad – but that's it.

Not all marriages work out. A man can get rid of his wife just by saying he's divorcing her, but a woman has to find an *archon* who will agree to act for her. And after she's divorced, everything stays with her ex-husband, including any children.

A woman's work

If you're staying with a Greek family, the mother will be very grateful if you offer to help out around the house. She has to spend all her time working: looking after children, making sure the house is always stocked up on supplies, keeping the place clean, getting meals ready on time, nursing sick relatives... So she'll certainly be able to find something for you to do.

With all that work, it's no surprise that women are mostly stuck at home. You won't see wealthy women in the streets - they only go to festivals and funerals. Poorer women have to go shopping and fetch water, but at least it gives them a chance to get some fresh air.

Fetching water – a great chance to catch up on the latest gossip

Mad about the boy

A wife's most important job of all is to give birth to healthy babies - preferably boys. Girls aren't allowed to inherit property, so most parents want at least one son, who'll be able to support them in old age. What's more, most boys will grow up to fight as hoplites, and help protect the city-state against invaders.

Second-hand babies

You might be shocked to hear that a father can reject his wife's baby if he doesn't want it. This usually happens if he thinks it isn't his, or if it's disabled, or if it's a girl, of course.

The rejected baby will normally just be taken out and abandoned. Some cities even have special places to leave these babies, who will then be brought up as slaves.

109

Schools & learning

It might not seem that much fun to tour a school while you're on holiday, but it's fascinating if you want to know what life's like for Ancient Greek children. Well, for boys from rich families, anyway. Girls aren't allowed to go, and schools charge fees that only the wealthy can afford.

Schools of thought

You might think one school at a time is enough, but not in Ancient Greece. Students have to go to three in a day - each teaching different subjects.

At the first, a teacher called a *grammatistes* teaches reading, writing and mathematics. Instead of books, boys write on waxed boards. The second school is for poetry and music, taught by a *kitharistes*. (You won't want to spend long here - a beginner playing the lyre doesn't sound great.) The third is for dancing and athletics, taught by a *paidotribes* at a *gymnasium* (training ground).

Boys go to school from the age of seven, and finish at eighteen to go into military training.

A *kitharistes* shows a student how to hold a lyre properly.

I have an idea!

Since you're from the 21st century, you probably know a lot about the world that the Ancient Greeks don't. So be very careful what you say – there are plenty of people who put everything down to the gods, and won't believe anything else.

But you might be surprised to see some of the amazing things that Greek scholars have worked out...

The only good thing is knowledge, and the only bad thing is ignorance.

Socrates, the famous philosopher, likes to get his teeth stuck into some knowledge.

Astronomy: an astronomer named Aristarchus has turned astronomy on its head by announcing that the Earth revolves around the Sun. Most Ancient Greeks think it's the other way round.

Pythagoras's scroll, full of exciting discoveries

History: the Persian Wars showed how handy it was to know all about your enemy. Now the Greeks love finding out about foreigners.

Mathematics: Pythagoras has some ground-breaking theories on triangles and circles.

Physics: In about 200 years, Archimedes will work out how to calculate an object's volume using water – while sitting in the bath.

Archimedes notices the water overflow when he gets in, and twigs that an object displaces its own volume of liquid.

Youngsters like to shock the old and fusty with high hemlines.

Tunics are sewn up at the sides and fastened on the shoulders.

This crimson *chlamys* is fastened with a brooch.

The *himation*: simply wrap and go for a dignified look.

Greek chic

A time tourist needs to have the right clothes. Wear a watch, or a baseball cap, and you'll attract unwanted attention. These pages will give you an idea what's acceptable.

First of all, the Greeks don't exactly dress to impress (except when they're getting ready for battle). Simplicity is the rule: a rectangle of material draped over the body as a cloak or tunic (rectangles are easy to weave). If you wear anything fancier, people will soon be gossiping about you at the local fountain.

Most people stick to wool in winter and linen in summer, but the rich splash out on silk or cotton (imported from India).

His...

In Ancient Greece it's the boys who show off their legs. Young men wear kilts or thigh-length tunics, leaving longer lengths for their elders and betters. Craftsmen and slaves often just wear loincloths. They're nice and cool for doing heavy work in.

If you want to mix with philosophers, get a *himation* (a wrap) to make yourself look extra wise. For travel, a short cloak called a *chlamys* is useful, and won't get in the way.

...and hers

Female time tourists will need a dress, called a *chiton* (if they're not dressing up as boys). There's a choice of Doric or Ionic. Both can be fastened with brooches, pins and belts. Women get *himations*, too - anything from a scarf to a cloak.

Doric: folded over at the top, then wrapped around the body.

Ionic: fastened along the arms at intervals.

A *himation*: this type is good for cold weather.

Fashion victims

Fashion changes all the time. Highly patterned *chitons* made of clinging material - recently fashion no-nos - are now popular again. To be at the forefront of this revival, look for a *chiton* in the finest cloth you can afford. If money's no object, you could even go for one with gold ornaments sewn in.

Weaving women

This picture of women weaving is taken from a painted vase. Women make all their own clothes – and their husband's and children's.

First the wool is spun by hand, and then it's woven on a loom. This work takes a long time, though rich women have slaves to help – or do all of it.

A fashionable *chiton* can attract some envious looks.

113

A trendy look for a typical man-about-town: neat and well groomed.

A fashionable lady's hairstyle can take quite a while to get right in the morning.

A good, tough pair of sandals should keep your feet cool in hot weather.

From top...

Men love hanging around at the barber's shop - they can catch up on the latest news and get their hair and beard trimmed at the same time. If you happen to pass one, you'll see it's a busy place.

Girls aren't allowed in, but they don't need a haircut very often anyway - most women grow their hair long. It still needs a lot of attention though. It's usually worn up, held in place with ribbons, scarves or nets. The only exceptions are slaves and women in mourning, who have their hair cut short.

Bad hair day or not, everyone wears hats outside to protect against the sun - and you should, too.

...to toe

Many people go barefoot. But the ground can get very hot in the middle of the day, so if you're not used to it, pick up a pair of leather sandals at the local market.

If you're thinking of going riding at some point, you might like to invest in a pair of calf-length boots. These are much sturdier than sandals, but don't wear them for long inside - you'll boil.

Accessorize!

Greek clothes might seem plain, but people make up for it by piling on loads of jewels: brooches, bracelets, necklaces, earrings and rings, for both men and women.

There are gold, silver and ivory pieces for the rich, and bronze, iron, lead, bone and glass for the poor. You won't see any diamond rings though – diamonds won't be used for years yet.

Creams and cosmetics

No self-respecting Greek woman would be seen dead in public without a thick layer of foundation. So there's a huge array of cosmetics and face creams on sale.

Don't be tempted to experiment yourself, though – you're better off sticking with toiletries from home. Not only are most Greek cosmetics horribly smelly, but face powder is full of powdered lead, which is highly poisonous. It gives new meaning to the phrase, "drop-dead gorgeous".

Golden touch

If you want to mix with wealthy Greeks, wear the most expensive and elaborate accessories you can afford. This gold earring is a good example. It's so intricate, it even includes a head wearing gold earrings of its own.

A Greek woman puts on her face powder.

Myths & legends

The Ancient Greeks are great storytellers. They love hearing about famous heroes, and use tales called myths to explain the world around them. Here are a few of them.

Pandora's box

Zeus created the very first woman out of clay and named her Pandora. He gave her a wonderful box, but forbade her ever to look inside. One day, Pandora's curiosity got too much and she lifted the lid. Out flew all the bad things of the world: sins, sickness and death. But people weren't left in despair, for the last item to fly from the box was hope.

Changing seasons

Demeter, goddess of the harvest, had a beautiful daughter, Persephone. Pluto saw her, fell in love and took her to Hades. Demeter was devastated and the crops went to ruin. Finally, Pluto compromised: he let Persephone out for six months each year. When Persephone is with her mother, spring arrives and the crops grow. When she goes back to Hades, it turns to winter.

Pluto wanted Persephone to stay in Hades all the time.

116

Flying & falling

A great inventor named Daedalus built a maze on Crete called the Labyrinth, to house a monster called the Minotaur. But then he fell out with the King and fled. He and his son Icarus flew to freedom on two pairs of home-made wings, made of wax and feathers. But Icarus flew too close to the sun. The wax melted, his wings fell apart, and he fell into the sea and drowned.

Theseus & the minotaur

Once a year, 14 Athenians were sent to Crete as food for the Minotaur. Theseus, prince of Athens, decided to put a stop to it. He told his father, Aegeus, that he would return under white sails if he was successful.

In Crete, he killed the Minotaur, and found his way back out of its maze using a ball of thread, given to him by an adoring princess who left Crete with him.

But Theseus repaid her kindness by dumping her on an island. To punish him, the gods made him forget his promise, and he sailed home under black sails. Thinking his son was dead, Aegeus threw himself off a cliff in despair.

Daedalus' adventures

The King of Crete tried to find Daedalus by issuing a challenge: to pass a thread through a spiral seashell. He knew that if anyone could do it, it would be the cunning Daedalus.

Sure enough, Daedalus succeeded by tying the thread to an ant, which walked through the shell. But he managed to escape the King once again.

The minotaur: half man, half bull, all monster

117

Top tips for tourists

No. 25: War stories

If you know no other Greek myths, make sure you know about the Trojan War. Greeks never get tired of hearing stories about it – the more gory, the better.

To get to grips with it, listen to a rhapsode perform *The Iliad* – an epic poem by Homer. It tells the story of the war, and is the most popular poem in all of Greece.

The Trojan War

It all began when Trojan prince Paris ran off with Helen, the wife of Menelaus, King of Sparta. Furious, Menelaus rounded up fellow Greek kings and launched a bloody ten-year war against the Trojans. In the end the Greeks pretended to go, leaving behind a present for their enemies - a wooden horse, secretly full of soldiers.

When the horse was inside Troy, the Greeks jumped out, let in their friends, and massacred the Trojans.

66 *Don't trust the horse, Trojans. Whatever it is, I fear the Greeks, even when they bring gifts.* 99

The Roman poet Virgil offers helpful advice – a little too late for the Trojans, though.

Journey of Odysseus

After a decade fighting the Trojan War, the Greek king Odysseus spent another ten years at sea, trying to get home. By the time he did, all his men were dead and other princes were after his wife Penelope. Odysseus, who was pretty fed up by now, killed them all and took back his kingdom.

Perseus & the gorgon

Perseus, a son of Zeus, was told to kill the gorgon Medusa. Not only did she have snakes where other people have hair, her glance turned men to stone. Athene gave Perseus a mirror so he didn't have to look directly into the gorgon's deadly eyes. Perseus managed to kill Medusa and gave her terrible head to Athene, who stuck it on her shield. (Which shows that, even where gods are concerned, there's no accounting for taste.)

Triumphant Perseus holds up Medusa's head.

Jason & the Argonauts

Jason was a prince who was denied his throne when he was just a baby by Pelias, his wicked uncle. When Jason grew up, Pelias agreed to let him have his throne back if he completed a dangerous quest.

He had to fetch the Golden Fleece, a gold sheepskin which hung in faraway Colchis, guarded by a dragon. Jason set sail in a ship called the *Argo*, along with his crew, the Argonauts. Like all Greek heroes, Jason was triumphant, albeit aided by the gods and an adoring princess (Medea, who even killed her own brother to help Jason).

Revenge of Medea

Just like Theseus, Jason made the mistake of abandoning his princess – and lived to regret it. Years after his adventures with the golden fleece, he tried to ditch Medea and marry another princess, Glaucis. Furious, Medea, sent Glaucis a wedding present: a magic robe, which burst into flames and killed her. Then she killed the children she had with Jason, and fled.

Famous people

Aeschylus (c.525-456BC): one of the best-known Greek playwrights, he's written over 80 tragedies. Only seven will survive, so catch one while you can. Known as the first writer to bring dialogue and action to the stage, his most famous work is a trilogy, called the *Oresteia*.

Alcibiades (c.450-404BC): politician brought up by Pericles, a brilliant but rowdy man and a troublemaker to be avoided at all costs. His pranks include vandalizing statues.

Anaxagoras (c.500-c.428BC): philosopher and friend of Pericles, whose theories on the universe will influence many other philosophers. Not only has he realized that the Sun is a ball of flames and the moon merely reflects light, he was the first to explain a solar eclipse.

Archimedes (c.287-212BC): inventor, mathematician and astronomer. As well as his famous bathtub discovery (which you can find out about on 111), he'll invent the screw pump, which is used to lift water uphill. He will be very popular with the army for building great war machines, including a solar-powered heat ray to burn enemy ships.

Aristeides (c.520-c.467BC): politician and general who is known as 'the Just' because he's so good, kind and fair. He's remembered for helping to set up the Delian League.

Aristophanes (c.445-c.385BC): famous Greek comic playwright and author of over 40 comedies. If tragedy isn't for you, try one of his shows, including *The Wasps*, *The Frogs* and *The Birds*. (Just don't expect animal documentaries.)

Aristotle (384-322BC): the best-known Greek philosopher, he'll study at the Academy, a school to be run by Plato. Aristotle will single-handedly invent a whole new science. Your biology lessons are thanks to him.

Aspasia (born c.456BC): Pericles' partner and mother of his son. You'll find plenty of people ready to mock her, just because she isn't from Athens. But she's beautiful, well-educated and counts Socrates as a friend.

Draco (7th century BC): politician who was appointed to improve the legal system and made it extremely harsh. Even laziness became a crime, punishable by death. Solon later abolished most of these "draconian" laws, however, so you can relax and enjoy a lazy holiday without being executed.

Euclid (lived c.300BC): important mathematician who'll write a summary of his predecessors' mathematical ideas. Some of his theories will still be followed in the 21st century.

Euripides (c.485-406BC): author of tragedies, he'll write over 90 plays and win five first prizes at the Athens Play Festival. Famous for his natural style and showing characters' inner feelings, he's been criticized for creating "evil" characters. But if you ask me, that just makes his plays more dramatic.

Herodotus (c.490-c.425BC): known as the "father of history", he's the first Greek to establish historical facts and work out why things happened in the way that they did.

Hippocrates (c.460-c.370BC): doctor who studies a patient's symptoms, seeking practical causes for illness rather than religious ones. 2,000 years later, doctors will still use his promise to treat patients well (the Hippocratic Oath) upon qualifying.

Homer (c.8th century BC): poet who recited epic tales from memory. His works include *The Iliad* and *The Odyssey*, which tell the story of the Trojan War and what happened afterwards to one of its heroes, Odysseus.

Lysias (c.445-c.380BC): cunning orator, extremely skilled at writing speeches. He's much in demand by people in need of a good defence in the law courts.

Myron (5th century BC): sculptor from Athens. Look out for his famous statue of a man throwing a discus – it will be copied many times.

Pericles (c.495-429BC): powerful Athenian politician, who'll be elected war commander for 14 years in a row. He's also the inspiration behind the rebuilding of the Acropolis in Athens.

Pheidias (c.490-c.432BC): artist who began as a painter and now sculpts. You can see his statues of Athene on the Acropolis and inside the Parthenon. But you'll have to go to Olympus to see his masterpiece: a vast statue of the god Zeus.

Pindar (c.518-c.438BC): the poet laureate of the day, he writes lengthy odes and hymns to great leaders and sporting heroes.

Plato (427-347BC): brilliant philosopher and pupil of Socrates, he'll set up a school called The Academy and write books on how to run an ideal state.

Praxiteles (born c.390BC): Athenian sculptor who will become famous for his statues of the gods, and develop a new delicate style, in contrast to the grand, formal style of sculptors before him. (He will also carve the first nude female statue.)

Pythagoras (c.580-c.500BC): philosopher and mathematician who lived with a large band of followers. His discoveries on right-angled triangles will last a lot longer than his peculiar ban on meat and beans.

Sappho (born c.612BC): female poet, who wrote nine books about love, family and friends.

Socrates (469-399BC):philosopher famous for being ugly yet charismatic, his mistake will be to point out the government's flaws. Accused of corrupting the young, he'll be sentenced to death by poison.

Solon (c.640BC-c.558BC): well-respected politician who introduced a more humane legal system and encouraged the development of trade and industry.

Sophocles (c.496-c.405BC): prize-winning author of tragedies, who is pioneering the use of stage scenery and is a politician in his spare time.

Thucydides (c.460-c.399BC): politician, writer and historian who will write a great book of military history.

Xenophon (c.428-c.354BC): writer and pupil of Socrates, he will fight for the Persians and Spartans against Athens, and will be banished to Sparta.

Timeline

Here is a timeline showing some of the biggest and most important events in Ancient Greek history. You never know, it could come in handy...

If you want to know more, remember to visit the Usborne Quicklinks Website (see page 6).

Spartan boys training

Early history

From 40000BC	Hunter-gatherers in Greece.
c.6500-3000BC	People start moving to Crete; potters set up shop in Greece and Crete.
c.6000BC	Farming takes off.

The Bronze Age

c.2900BC	Population booms in Greece; towns are established; metalworkers set up beside potters.
c.2500BC	The city of Troy is built.
c.2000BC	The first Greeks to speak the Greek language identified in Greece.
c.1900BC	On Crete, the Minoans civilization is flourishing.
c.1600BC	The Mycenaeans become top dogs in Greece.
c.1450BC	Crete and the Minoans are overrun by Mycenaeans who go from strength to strength.
c.1250BC	The city of Mycenae fortified; the Trojan War (probably) breaks out.
c.1200BC	The Mycenaean civilization is in decline.

The Dark Ages

By 1100BC	The Mycenaeans lose everything, including knowing how to read and write. New style of writing introduced in the Archaic Period.
c.850-750BC	The poet Homer is born, lives and dies around now.

The Archaic Period

c.800BC	The Greeks, especially traders, start getting in contact with the outside world again.
776BC	The first-ever Olympic Games are held in Olympia (probably).
c.740-720BC	The Spartans start coming on heavy, conquering the nearby state of Messenia.
c.650BC	Tyrants seize power in Greece.
c.630-613BC	The Messenians stand up to the Spartans but are knocked back down.
c.621BC	Draco comes to power in Athens, laying down draconian laws.
c.594BC	Sighs of relief as Solon becomes archon and changes most of Draco's laws.
508BC	Cleisthenes takes over and introduces democracy – of sorts.
500-499BC	Greek colonies in Ionia turn against their Persian rulers.
490BC	The Persians are defeated at the battle of Marathon.
480BC	Persians beat the Greeks at Thermopylae and Greeks beat the Persians at Salamis.
479BC	The Persians are finally defeated and kicked out of Greece.

The Classical Era

Sculptor at work

c.500–336BC	Greek art has its Classical Period.
478BC	The Delian League is formed by Athens and allies against the Persians.
461–429BC	Pericles is the politician of the moment (for 33 years).
460–457BC	The Long Walls go up; the Acropolis is rebuilt after the Persians left it in ruins.
449BC	The Delian League agrees a truce with Persia.
445BC	30 Years' Peace is declared between Athens and Sparta. But a decade later...
431–404BC	The Athenians and Spartans are fighting the Peloponnesian Wars.
430BC	A plague hits Athens.
421BC	Athens and Sparta agree to keep the peace for 50 years. (Sound familiar?)
420BC	Alcibiades becomes leader of Athens.
413BC	Athens and Sparta are fighting again.
407–404BC	Three successive victories for the Spartans. The Long Walls are knocked down; the Delian League is dissolved; democracy packs up and leaves Athens.
403BC	Democracy comes back.
399BC	War between Sparta and Persia. Socrates is sentenced to death by poison.
395–387BC	Corinth, Athens, Argos and Thebes battle Sparta which is still fighting Persia.
394BC	The Spartans lose to the Persians.
394–391BC	The Long Walls are rebuilt.
387BC	The Spartans lose to everyone else.
338BC	Philip II of Macedon conquers Greece. Independent city-states are history.

The Hellenistic Age

Roman soldier

336–323BC	Philip's son, Alexander, founds an empire which stretches from Greece all the way to India. It breaks up on his (untimely) death.
323–322BC	The city-states fight for their independence, but don't get it.
From 323BC on	Greek states are ruled by descendants of Alex's generals.
202–197BC	Philip V of Greece hands the country over to the Romans – not without a fight, but one he loses.
147–146BC	Direct Roman rule is imposed on the whole of Greece.

Glossary

acropolis: fortified hill top

agora: market and meeting place

amphora (plural: *amphorae*): large pot which holds liquids

andron: men's dining room

cella: main room in a temple

chiton: woman's dress

choregos: a wealthy man who pays for a dramatic production

citizen: free man with the right to vote

democracy: political system in which all citizens have a say in running their state

grammatistes: teacher

gynaeceum: women's quarters in a house

Hellene: the name that the Greeks give themselves

herm: a bust on a stone pillar; herms of the god Hermes are often placed ouside homes.

hetaira (plural: *hetairai*): woman who entertains men at parties

himation: cloak or shawl

hoplite: heavily-armed foot soldier

kylix: a shallow drinking cup

krater: large vase for holding wine and water

mystery cult: religious cult with strict rules of entry

ostracism: vote to banish politicians

paidagogos: slave or hired chaperone who takes boys to and from lessons

philosopher: scholar who questions the world around him

Pythia: the priestess who delivers messages from Apollo

relief: carving on a stone panel

rhapsode: man who recites poetry

soothsayer: someone thought able to predict the future

sophist: teacher of public speaking

stoa: roofed passageway with columns

symposium: dinner party for men

trireme: warship with three tiers of rowers

Underworld (Hades): kingdom of the dead

Index

Acknowledgements:
Red-figured wine cooler, page 67 © The British Museum/Heritage Images

Cover designed by Karen Tomlins
Digital manipulation by Keith Furnival

Edited by Jane Chisholm
History consultant: Dr. Anne Millard

This edition first published in 2013 by Usborne Publishing Ltd.,
Usborne House, 83-85 Saffron Hill, London EC1N 8RT, England.
www.usborne.com
Copyright © 2013, 2009, 2008, 2003 Usborne Publishing Ltd.
The name Usborne and the devices ♀♥ are Trade Marks of Usborne Publishing Ltd.